DATE DUE

MY 29 01		
NO 9 01		
JY 06 02		
AR 10 03		
MY 19 03		
X T R		
9-23-03		
JY 18 04		
AG 4 05		
FE 28 07		
12 27		

GAYLORD   PRINTED IN U.S.A.

THE WAY PEOPLE LIVE

Life on Ellis Island

Life on
Ellis Island

Titles in The Way People Live series include:

Cowboys in the Old West
Games of Ancient Rome
Life Among the Great Plains Indians
Life Among the Ibo Women of Nigeria
Life Among the Indian Fighters
Life Among the Pirates
Life Among the Samurai
Life Among the Vikings
Life as a Hitler Youth
Life During the Ancient Roman Games
Life During the Black Death
Life During the Crusades
Life During the French Revolution
Life During the Gold Rush
Life During the Great Depression
Life During the Jim Crow Laws
Life During the Middle Ages
Life During the Renaissance
Life During the Russian Revolution
Life During the Spanish Inquisition
Life in a Japanese American Internment Camp
Life in a Medieval Castle
Life in Ancient Athens
Life in Ancient Greece
Life in Ancient Rome
Life in an Amish Colony
Life in an Eskimo Village
Life in a Wild West Show
Life in Charles Dickens's England
Life in Communist Russia
Life in the Amazon Rain Forest
Life in the American Colonies
Life in the Elizabethan Theater
Life in the Hitler Youth
Life in the North During the Civil War
Life in the South During the Civil War
Life in the Warsaw Ghetto
Life in Victorian England
Life in War-Torn Bosnia
Life of a Roman Slave
Life of a Slave on a Southern Plantation
Life on a Medieval Pilgrimage
Life on an African Slave Ship
Life on an Israeli Kibbutz
Life on Ellis Island
Life on the American Frontier
Life on the Oregon Trail
Life on the Underground Railroad
Life Under the Jim Crow Laws

THE WAY PEOPLE LIVE

Life on
Ellis Island

by Renee C. Rebman

Lucent Books, P.O. Box 289011, San Diego, CA 92198-9011

Library of Congress Cataloging-in-Publication Data

Rebman, Renee C., 1961–
    Life on Ellis Island / by Renee C. Rebman.
        p.   cm. — (The way people live)
    Includes bibliographical references and index.
    Summary: Discusses life on Ellis Island, including detainment and de-
portation of immigrants, daily activities, the development of the immigration
station, its role in the formation of the great melting pot of America, and the
later years.
    ISBN 1-56006-533-8 (lib. bdg.: alk. paper)
    1. Ellis Island Immigration Station (N.Y. and N.J.)—History Juvenile
literature.   [1. Ellis Island Immigration Station (N.Y. and N.J.)—History.
2. United States—Emigration and immigration.]
I. Title.   II. Series.
  JV6484.R42   2000
  325.73'09—dc21   99-30876
                                                                          CIP

To the memory of my grandfather, Henry Gentille,
and of my great-grandparents who came to this country
from Italy, Yugoslavia, and Austria

Contents

Discovering the Humanity in Us All

Books in The Way People Live series focus on groups of people in a wide variety of circumstances, settings, and time periods. Some books focus on different cultural groups, others, on people in a particular historical time period, while others cover people involved in a specific event. Each book emphasizes the daily routines, personal and historical struggles, and achievements of people from all walks of life.

To really understand any culture, it is necessary to strip the mind of the common notions we hold about groups of people. These stereotypes are the archenemies of learning. It does not even matter whether the stereotypes are positive or negative; they are confining and tight. Removing them is a challenge that's not easily met, as anyone who has ever tried it will admit. Ideas that do not fit into the templates we create are unwelcome visitors—ones we would prefer remain quietly in a corner or forgotten room.

The cowboy of the Old West is a good example of such confining roles. The cowboy was courageous, yet soft-spoken. His time (it is always a he, in our template) was spent alternatively saving a rancher's daughter from certain death on a runaway stagecoach, or shooting it out with rustlers. At times, of course, he was likely to get a little crazy in town after a trail drive, but for the most part, he was the epitome of inner strength. It is disconcerting to find out that the cowboy is human, even a bit childish. Can it really be true that cowboys would line up to help the cook on the trail drive grind coffee, just hoping he would give them a little stick of peppermint candy that came with the coffee shipment? The idea of tough cowboys vying with one another to help "Coosie" (as they called their cooks) for a bit of candy seems silly and out of place.

So is the vision of Eskimos playing video games and watching MTV, living in prefab housing in the Arctic. It just does not fit with what "Eskimo" means. We are far more comfortable with snow igloos and whale blubber, harpoons and kayaks.

Although the cultures dealt with in Lucent's The Way People Live series are often historically and socially well known, the emphasis is on the personal aspects of life. Groups of people, while unquestionably affected by their politics and their governmental structures, are more than those institutions. How do people in a particular time and place educate their children? What do they eat? And how do they build their houses? What kinds of work do they do? What kinds of games do they enjoy? The answers to these questions bring these cultures to life. People's lives are revealed in the particulars and only by knowing the particulars can we understand these cultures' will to survive and their moments of weakness and greatness.

This is not to say that understanding politics does not help to understand a culture. There is no question that the Warsaw ghetto, for example, was a culture that was brought about by the politics and social ideas of Adolf

Hitler and the Third Reich. But the Jews who were crowded together in the ghetto cannot be understood by the Reich's politics. Their life was a day-to-day battle for existence, and the creativity and methods they used to prolong their lives is a vital story of human perseverance that would be denied by focusing only on the institutions of Hitler's Germany. Knowing that children as young as five or six outwitted Nazi guards on a daily basis, that Jewish policemen helped the Germans control the ghetto, that children attended secret schools in the ghetto and even earned diplomas—these are the things that reveal the fabric of life, that can inspire, intrigue, and amaze.

Books in The Way People Live series allow both the casual reader and the student to see humans as victims, heroes, and onlookers. And although humans act in ways that can fill us with feelings of sorrow and revulsion, it is important to remember that "hero," "predator," and "victim" are dangerous terms. Heaping undue pity or praise on people reduces them to objects, and strips them of their humanity.

Seeing the Jews of Warsaw only as victims is to deny their humanity. Seeing them only as they appear in surviving photos, staring at the camera with infinite sadness, is limiting, both to them and to those who want to understand them. To an object of pity, the only appropriate response becomes "Those poor creatures!" and that reduces both the quality of their struggle and the depth of their despair. No one is served by such two-dimensional views of people and their cultures.

With this in mind, The Way People Live series strives to flesh out the traditional, two-dimensional views of people in various cultures and historical circumstances. Using a wide variety of primary quotations—the words not only of the politicians and government leaders, but of the real people whose lives are being examined—each book in the series attempts to show an honest and complete picture of a culture removed from our own by time or space.

By examining cultures in this way, the reader will notice not only the glaring differences from his or her own culture, but also will be struck by the similarities. For indeed, people share common needs—warmth, good company, stability, and affirmation from others. Ultimately, seeing how people really live, or have lived, can only enrich our understanding of ourselves.

Island of Hope, Island of Tears

B etween 1892 and 1954, more than 12 million people entered the United States through the Ellis Island immigration station, a processing complex in New York Harbor. During peak immigration periods more than four thousand immigrants were housed on Ellis Island at a time. How to process this crush of humanity boggled the minds of politicians and tested the skills and tempers of inspectors, interpreters, doctors, and overworked manual laborers who struggled to feed, care for, and accommodate them.

The Statue of Liberty was a promise of hope for many who came to America escaping economic hardship, famine, religious persecution, and war.

Island of Hope

Marta Forman, a Czechoslovakian immigrant who arrived at Ellis Island in 1922, was delighted and amazed by her experience, as she relates in *Ellis Island, Echoes from a Nation's Past*, edited by Susan Jonas.

"So when I came to Ellis Island, my gosh, there was something I'll never forget. The first impression—all kinds of nationalities. And the first meal we got—fish and milk, big pitchers of milk and white bread, the first time I saw white bread and butter. There was so much milk, and I drank it because we didn't have enough milk in my country. And I said, "My God, we're going to have a good time here. We're going to have plenty to eat.""

Immigrants receiving milk.

A Promise of Hope

The brave and often desperate people who crowded Ellis Island came from all over the world in hope of finding a better life in a country where many had been told the streets were paved with gold. Many were escaping economic hardship, famine, religious persecution, or war. For more than forty years they poured onto our nation's shores leaving everything familiar for a chance at the American dream and the welcome promised in Emma Lazarus's poem "The New Colossus":

Give me your tired, your poor,
Your huddled masses yearning to
    breathe free,
The wretched refuse of your teeming
    shore,
Send these, the homeless, tempest-tost
    to me,
I lift my lamp beside the golden door![1]

Lazarus's words, inscribed at the base of the Statue of Liberty, offer an unconditional acceptance of immigrants and an enthusiastic reception. However, what immigrants first

The Great Hall on Ellis Island saw more than 12 million immigrants pass through its doors.

encountered was not a warm welcome, but interviews, physical examinations, and long delays.

Ellis Island was the most well known immigration station in the world. Much more than a simple processing center or quick waiting station, the island operated as a small, self-contained city. Like all cities, it was the backdrop of the human drama of heartbreak and hope, birth, illness, marriage, and death on a daily basis.

The many buildings on Ellis Island included hospitals, sleeping quarters, a dining hall, library, school, recreation center, railroad ticket office, post office, telegraph office, money exchange, morgue, baggage room, laundry, and courtrooms. The Registry Room, known as the Great Hall, was an awe-inspiring two hundred feet long and one hundred feet wide, with a fifty-six-foot-high vaulted ceiling. Stories of the Great Hall and the impressive architecture of Ellis Island crossed the ocean to the immigrants' homelands and were passed down from generation to generation.

Architectural Riches

Rosanne Welch, granddaughter of Giuseppe Italiano, an Italian immigrant who came through Ellis Island in 1904, recalls how her grandfather felt when he saw the buildings on Ellis Island: "I remember my grandfather always telling me how he knew he could be rich in America because he saw riches in the architecture of Ellis Island. He felt that if they let the poor in such a gorgeous hall then life in this country was just."[2]

The Great Hall was also a confusing and frightening place as the babble of foreign tongues rose to excited crescendos. It was a never-ending challenge for doctors, translators, baggage handlers, and officials to deal with uncomprehending, fatigued, and worried immigrants. Language barriers only intensified the turmoil inherent in overcrowding. An incoming immigrant spent, on average, a total of five hours on Ellis Island, but for the detainee the visit stretched to days, weeks, or even months.

Overcrowding, instances of abuse, miscommunication, endless delays, and the heartbreak of the thousands who were refused entry and deported gave Ellis Island a reputation as an island of tears. But many employees, social workers, and immigration commissioners made sincere and even Herculean efforts to help immigrants in their passage through the island. Eighteen languages were interpreted. Every effort was made to locate sponsoring relatives for the newcomers, who sometimes arrived with incomplete addresses and sketchy information on the whereabouts of family members already in the United States. Religious services were conducted in the Catholic, Protestant, and

"Everybody Has Tears"

For Fannie Kligerman, a Russian immigrant who came to Ellis Island in 1905, the island was a sad place. She tells her story in David Brownstone's *Island of Hope, Island of Tears.*

"Everybody was sad there. There was not a smile on anybody's face. Here they thought maybe they wouldn't go through. There they thought maybe my child won't go through. There was such a sadness, no smile any place. You could see. . . . That's when I came here in 1905. The people had such terrible sad faces. Such a sad place there.

Oh, did I cry. Terribly. When you cry and I can see how you cry, I cry, too. All my sisters and brothers cried. So I cried. You don't know why you cry. Just so much sadness there that you have to cry. But there's more tears in Ellis Island to ten people than, say, to a hundred people elsewhere. There is all of these tears, everybody has tears."

Fear of deportation and detainment lead many immigrants to tears and sadness.

Although some immigrants experienced hard times on Ellis Island, America was still a promise of hope.

Jewish faiths. In later years, movies and free concerts were offered regularly, a school was provided for detained children, and a free library was available to all.

Unending Memories

The stories of Ellis Island continue to be told, some of hope, some of tears. The Ellis Island immigrants have never forgotten their experience.

Theodore Lubik, an immigrant who arrived from Ukraine in 1913 and later became an employee of the island, gives a disarmingly simple explanation of the Ellis Island experience: "What was Ellis Island like? It was hell and it was good. For one who passed by, everything was all right. For one who was detained or sent back, oh, that was awful."[3]

CHAPTER 1

Coming to America

The great immigration movement began in Europe in the 1890s as working-class and poor families, hearing tales of plentiful jobs for themselves and free education for their children, decided to journey to America for a better life. These decisions were fueled by letters received from friends or relatives in the United States describing their new jobs and urging those at home to follow them. Although immigrants also struggled to survive in America, they did have more opportunities and hope for a brighter future. One Italian

European immigrants crowd the deck of the ship taking them to America.

immigrant remembered receiving letters from America: "In my little village only the priest could read or write. Whenever anyone received an 'America letter' from an uncle or a cousin the whole village would gather at the church to hear the priest read it."[4]

Families determined to make the journey slowly scraped money together for steamship tickets. For many, passage for an entire family traveling together was impossibly expensive, so someone, usually a father, would plan to go first, get a job, and send money back home to bring his family members to America. Sometimes, parents unwilling to leave the life they knew saved money to buy a ticket for their oldest son or daughter to venture across the Atlantic Ocean. These separations were often permanent. Once a peasant left his village, he rarely if ever returned. A Russian teenager recalls leaving his mother and father at a train station in a small Russian town: "When the train drew into the station my mother lost control of her feelings. As she embraced me for the last time her sobs became violent and Father had to separate us. There was despair in her way of clinging to me which I could not understand then. I understand it now. I never saw her again."[5]

The High Cost of Tickets

Steamship fare to America was expensive, but early-twentieth-century immigrants had no other travel option. Most immigrants could afford to purchase only steerage, or third-class, tickets. The steerage area comprised the decks below sea level where the steering mechanisms were located. In 1910 a steerage ticket cost ten to fifteen dollars. Second-class tickets were about twenty dollars more and first-class tickets could cost up to three times the price of steerage tickets.

Checked and Tagged

Transporting immigrants, by the millions, was the lifeblood of many steamship companies. Although no laws guaranteed immigrant rights or regulated their treatment, the steamship companies were required to examine the immigrants for disease. The companies were also required to vaccinate the immigrants against known diseases and disinfect them for lice before they sailed for America. The steamship companies had to shoulder the expenses involved if U.S. officials found reason to deport an immigrant, including the cost of the return trip. Thus the steamship companies were motivated to comply with health screening, and passengers received a detailed and careful examination before they were allowed to purchase a ticket.

Each immigrant was thoroughly examined by a doctor to determine if he or she had a disease or condition that would prohibit admission to the United States. Men and boys often had their hair shorn very closely by the doctors to prevent lice and the women and girls were examined carefully to make sure they were free of the vermin.

The steamship company also prepared a detailed report, called a manifest, which listed the name of every person on board along with important information including age, sex, marital status, occupation, nationality, race, place of birth, height, complexion, color of hair and eyes, marks of identification, and purpose of travel to the United States. Passengers had large identification tags pinned to their clothing before boarding which stated their ultimate U.S. destination. Inspectors on Ellis Island used the ship's manifest to compare and verify the information on the immigrant's tag. Unlisted or untagged passengers were suspected of being stowaways. If this was found to be the case, they were immediately deported.

Immigrants wore large identification tags pinned to their clothing stating their ultimate destination in America.

Steerage Accommodations

While passengers traveling first or second class had cabins, clean bed linens, sumptuous meals served in dining rooms, and free dances with live music, those in steerage endured inhumane conditions. Operators of the largest ships could, and often did, pack one thousand immigrants into steerage. The compartment was damp and bunks were tightly stacked in tiers. Ventilation, fresh water, and adequate restroom facilities did not exist. The food was sparse and often infested with maggots. Men were separated from women and children. Only during fine weather were steerage passengers allowed to go to an upper deck for fresh air and a little exercise or socializing.

In 1911 an investigator for the U.S. Immigration Commission posed as an immigrant and sailed in steerage. She later wrote of the conditions:

When the steerage is full, each passenger's space is limited to his berth, which then serves as bed, clothes and towel rack, cupboard, and baggage space. . . . There was no hook on which to hang a garment, no receptacle for refuse . . . no cans for use in case of seasickness. . . . No woman with the smallest degree of modesty, and with no other conveniences than a wash room, used jointly with men, and a faucet of cold salt water can keep clean amidst such surroundings for a period of twelve days and more. . . .

[The eating utensils] consist of a fork, a large spoon, and a combination working-man's tin lunch pail. The bottom or pail part is used for soup and frequently as a wash basin; a small tin dish that fits into the top of the pails used for meat and potatoes; a cylindrical projection on the lid is a dish for vegetables or stewed fruits; a tin cup that fits onto this projection is for drinks. These must serve the passenger throughout the voyage. . . . The dishes are soon rusty, and not fit to eat from.[6]

Seasickness was a common malady; more serious diseases such as typhus (a severe infectious disease often transmitted by body lice and causing a high fever, delirium, and stupor) also spread rapidly in the crowded conditions and often killed dozens on a single voyage. The dead were unceremoniously buried at sea.

Nine-year-old Dominick Piccolo witnessed such an incident aboard ship during his voyage from Italy:

> We have a storm at sea. Lightning, thunder, the waves like mountains. The ship is rocking. I fall on my nose. I start bleeding. [One] woman—her husband is sick. During the night, he dies. They give him the prayers. Then they throw him overboard. His wife is screaming, "My husband! My husband!"[7]

The Statue of Liberty

The Statue of Liberty made an indelible impression on immigrants as they entered New York Harbor. Theodore Spako, who traveled to the United States in 1911 at the age of sixteen, recalls the confused conversation he had with shipboard friends about the identity of the great statue in Peter Coan's book *Ellis Island Interviews*.

"We landed in New York after twenty-two days at sea. I remember we see Statue of Liberty. Gus ask me, 'What's the statue?' And then we're looking at the statue, and his father say, 'That's Christopher Columbus.' And I put my two cents out. I say, 'Listen, this don't look like Christopher Columbus. That's a lady there.'"

The Lady with the Torch

After an arduous journey lasting from ten days to three weeks, the sight of the Statue of Liberty standing proud in the waters of New York Harbor drew shouts of joy from the crowds on the ship's decks. Many cried with relief or offered prayers of thanks. Some stood in awed silence. Almost all had heard about the statue and knew it meant they had finally made it to America.

Class Discrimination

When the steamship arrived in New York Harbor, first- and second-class passengers were

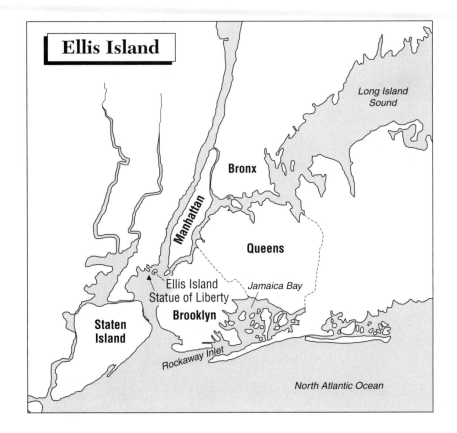

Ellis Island

Long Island Sound

Bronx

Manhattan

Queens

Ellis Island
Statue of Liberty

Jamaica Bay

Brooklyn

Staten Island

Rockaway Inlet

North Atlantic Ocean

examined quickly on board by U.S. immigration inspectors. Very few were made to go through processing on Ellis Island. They then disembarked onto waiting ferries and were allowed to pass directly into New York. Third-class steerage passengers, deemed more likely to be diseased or undesirable, were automatically required to go through lengthy inspection on Ellis Island. Because the Ellis Island facility could only process about five thousand new immigrants a day, immigrants sometimes had to wait their turn aboard ship until previous shiploads of immigrants had been cleared through the island. The discriminatory nature of the disembarkation is clear in U.S. immigration records from 1905, which show that of one hundred thousand first- and second-class passengers examined on board, only three thousand were required to pass through Ellis

Island. In contrast, during the same year the entire total of over eight hundred thousand steerage passengers were required to go through the island for processing.

Complacent Cattle

Without protest, the immigrants boarded small wooden ferries that took them to Ellis Island. One journalist remembered witnessing their slow progress as they lined up for the final leg of their journey toward a new life: "Their stolid faces hide frightened, throbbing hearts. They obey the signs, gestures, and directions of the attendants as dumbly as cattle, and as patiently."[8]

When the immigrants reached the island, their first task was to make their way to the

A Race to the Finish

The 1921 quota law stated that no more than 20 percent of the annual quota of immigrants from a particular country could be admitted in any one month, causing steamship companies to run dangerous risks in order to arrive in time to deliver their immigrants before the limit was reached. In Wilton Tifft's book *Ellis Island,* Henry Curran, commissioner at Ellis Island in 1923, describes the situation.

"Competing steamship companies would bring in immigrants from all over the world, trusting to win the race at the finish. It was dangerous to human life to have twenty great ships crowding through the Narrows at the stroke of midnight. It was a tragedy to the immigrants who had pulled up stakes, left home behind, and come hopefully here only to be turned back at the gate, through no fault of their own, as 'excess quota.' They had no place to go—the old home gone, the new home forbidden—it was tragedy that tore the heartstrings of those of us who understood."

baggage room on the ground floor. They were encouraged to check their baggage for the duration of the lengthy inspection process, but many refused, fearing their only worldly belongings would be lost or stolen. Instead, they dragged suitcases, bundles, and trunks with them as Ellis Island staff passed out food (sandwiches, fruit, doughnuts, cookies, and milk). Peter Mossini recalls savoring his first meal on the island:

When we reach New York, I thank the good Lord. It was early morning, the

Fourth of July. We was on the deck like a bunch of sheep. Everybody had a suitcase, dragging their suitcase, and I remember the first meal they gave to us at Ellis Island. They give a sandwich, white bread with a piece of cheese and a piece of ham and it tasted so good. It tasted like a nice piece of cake. That was something new for me. I never seen sandwiches in Sicily.[9]

Treasures from Home

The possessions the immigrants brought across the Atlantic included many unusual items and family treasures. Sentimentality sometimes overrode practicality when it came to choosing what to bring: Bibles, prayer books, family documents, and photographs were common items that nearly all immigrants carried with them. Beautiful handmade embroidered costumes were also packed carefully or worn on the trip. Many immigrants unable to fit all they wished to bring into their tattered suitcases wore several layers of clothing during the entire journey.

For Abraham Burstein, a Russian Jewish immigrant, packing was a relatively simple task: "I arrived in New York in 1921—all my belongings consisted of an additional change of underwear and two books."[10]

Women sometimes brought elaborate wedding gowns, either as precious heirlooms or to be worn for an impending wedding, as they expected to be met by a fiancé on arrival. Feather pillows and handmade linens were also brought in great quantities as they were considered too valuable to be left behind in the old country. Fannie Shook, a Polish Jewish immigrant, was very proud of the bedding her family brought with them. "What did we take with us? Our clothes, our pillows, our big, thick comforters made from pure goose feathers—not chicken feathers—and a barrel of pickles."[11]

Quantities of food (cheese, sausages, homemade butter, bread, and bottles of liquor) were commonly brought along either to be eaten during the journey or as gifts from home for waiting relatives.

The Medical Examination Begins

From the baggage room, the immigrants then labored up a long flight of stairs to the second floor, carrying their precious bundles and baggage. They did not know it, but their medical examination had begun. Doctors watched the immigrants carefully from the top of the stairs for signs that could reveal a medical problem. E. H. Mullan, a surgeon for the U.S. Public Health Service, describes the line inspection process:

> As the immigrant approaches the officer gives him a quick glance. Experience enables him in that one glance to take in six details, namely, the scalp, face, neck, hands, gait, and general condition, both mental and physical. Should any of these details not come into view, the alien is halted and the officer satisfies himself that no suspicious sign or symptom exists

Immigrants brought almost all of their personal possessions along with them to America.

Hot Water, Fond Memories

Many immigrants were fascinated and thrilled by the modern conveniences they encountered for the first time in their lives on Ellis Island. George Mardikian, a Greek immigrant quoted in Wilton S. Tifft's book *Ellis Island*, came to Ellis Island in 1922. He recalls his very first shower with joy.

"I began to sing. I stopped singing to splash and laugh, and then sang some more. The song and the beautiful, plentiful hot water were washing away the sweat and dust and grime of the steerage. I scrubbed harder and harder. I washed away the grime, I washed away the years. I washed away the Old World. I washed away all the hatred and injustice and cruelty I had known, all the hunger, all the weeping, all the pain."

regarding that particular detail. For instance, if the immigrant is wearing a high collar, the officer opens the collar or unbuttons the upper shirt button and sees whether a goiter, tumor, or other abnormality exists. . . . Likewise, if the alien approaches the officer with hat on he must be halted, hat removed and scalp observed in order to exclude the presence of favus [a highly contagious scalp disease], ringworm, or other skin diseases of this region of the body. Pompadours are always a suspicious sign. Beneath such long growth of hair are frequently seen areas of favus. . . . Where the alien carries luggage on his shoulder or back, it may be necessary to make him drop his parcels and to

walk 5 or 10 feet in order to exclude suspicious gait or spinal curvature. Immigrants at times carry large parcels in both arms and over their shoulders in order that the gait resulting from shortened extremity or ankylosed [fused or stiffened] joint may escape notice. In like manner they maneuver in attempting to conceal gaits of Little's disease, spastic paralysis, and other nervous disorders. All children over 2 years of age are taken from their mother's arms and are made to walk.[12]

Coded Chalk Marks

A chalk mark drawn on the shoulder of an immigrant's jacket or on his lapel indicated a wide variety of abnormalities. This system of coded chalk marks quickly identified immigrants needing further examination. Illness and medical problems were the most frequent causes of deportation. More than a dozen letters were used to indicate possible problems; for example, B: back, CT: trachoma, E: eyes, H: heart, L: lameness, Pg: pregnancy, Sc: scalp, X: suspected mental illness (a circled X meant definite signs of mental disease had been observed).

The immigrants did not know what the chalk markings meant. One woman recalls that a kindly stranger helped keep her sister from being taken away for further examination and possible deportation:

My sister developed warts on the back of her hand so they put a chalk X on the back of her coat. The Xs were put aside to see whether they had to be reexamined or deported. If they deported my sister we couldn't let her go. Where would she go if they deported her? Some kind man, I don't know who he was, told my sister to turn her coat around. She had a nice plush coat with a silk lining, and they turned her coat around.[13]

The Buttonhook Test

For the most part, unless marked for further examination, doctors conducted visual evaluations. Hands-on examinations followed if an initial chalk marking was made. By far the most dreaded part of the medical exam was the buttonhook test to check for trachoma, a contagious eye disease that can lead to blindness. This painful examination consisted of turning the eyelids inside-out with a buttonhook, an instrument meant to loop buttons on shoes. Evidence of trachoma was one of the

The painful buttonhook test consisted of turning the eyelids inside out with an instrument meant to loop buttons onto shoes.

In Peter Coan's book *Ellis Island Interviews,* Emanuel "Manny" Stein recalls a racket operated by two men supposedly aiding immigrants who did not have the necessary amount of money to be admitted.

"Afterwards, [when the physical exam was completed] we had customs immigration and we had to show our financial security of twenty dollars. I didn't realize until sometime later, but what happened was a lot of the guys on the ship were gambling. Some of the guys lost their twenty dollars. But there was a little racket there, you see. There was a wire fence and you had to go through the customs officers there. Now in order to go through you had to show your twenty dollars. But a little further back on the fence, there were a couple of guys making money. They would loan you the twenty dollars. Cost you two bucks, follow me? And they would loan you a twenty-dollar bill and you'd go to the gate and come through the gate, and the guy would be there to take the twenty-dollar bill back from you. Cost you two bucks. For two bucks you could show twenty. Whether the guy was splitting it with the guard I don't know."

most prevalent medical reasons for immigrant deportation.

Immigrants were also required to open their clothing so doctors could check for skin and venereal diseases. These examinations were embarrassing and devastating to the painfully shy immigrants, especially the women, who had most likely never been examined before. In later years, women served as attendants to help ease the fears of female immigrants.

Immigrants who were marked with chalk and pulled from the group were distressed and frightened that they might never see their families again. After the more complete medical examinations were finished and the results noted, healthy immigrants were returned to the main group to continue their processing.

After the immigrants had gone through all the steps of the medical examinations, they were herded into the Great Hall to await legal inspection. The Great Hall was divided by iron railings and wire into sections that resembled cattle pens. (After 1911 the railings were replaced by long wooden benches.) The immigrants slowly worked their way through the maze toward the west end of the room where legal examinations (a series of questions) were conducted.

Twenty-Nine Questions to Freedom

The legal inspectors sat at high desks at the end of the Great Hall with interpreters nearby. Immigrants were called forward in groups of thirty, the number of names listed on each ship's manifest card. The legal inspectors then fired off twenty-nine questions to each immigrant covering such issues as age, name, financial status, where they were going, who paid for their passage, if they had any relatives in America, and whether they had a job waiting for them. The proper answer to the last question was no. Although immigrants had to prove they were capable of supporting themselves and were not likely to become a public charge, they would most likely be deported if it was found that they had already made employment arrangements. The contract labor law of 1885 made it illegal for businesses to import immigrants with the intention of giving them jobs. This common practice had been used in previous years to import thousands of immigrants to work for very low wages in the railroad industry, steel mills, and coal mines. It was outlawed in response to public outcry that lower-paid immigrants were taking jobs away from American workers.

Immigrants were also required to show they had some money in their possession, usually twenty-five dollars, an arbitrary amount set by the commissioner of immigration. This was a large sum to an impoverished immigrant, who might have saved for more than a year. Anyone without the required funds could be detained until friends or relatives sent the money to them at Ellis Island.

During rush periods inspectors were overwhelmed by the sheer number of people waiting to be questioned. Interpreter Frank Martocci remembers the grueling pace of his work:

> Three or four times a week, from nine o'-clock in the morning to nine o'clock in the evening, we were continuously examining aliens. I thought it was a stream that would never end. Every twenty-four hours from three to five thousand people came before us, and I myself examined from four to five hundred a day. We were simply swamped by the human tide.[14]

The Literacy Test

Over the decades, increasingly strict legislation regarding inspection procedures, in part adopted under anti-immigration pressure, made it increasingly more difficult for an immigrant to enter the United States. The 1917 Immigration Act included legislation that made a literacy test mandatory; each immigrant had to be able to read a passage of at least forty words in their own language. Although President Woodrow Wilson vetoed the law on the grounds that it excluded "those to whom the opportunities of elementary education had been denied, without regard to their character, their purpose, or their natural capacity,"[15] Congress overrode the president's veto and the law remained in force until 1952.

Arnold Weiss, a Russian Jewish immigrant who came to the United States in 1921 at the age of thirteen, recalls how he helped his mother, who could not read, pass the test:

> They also questioned people on literacy. My uncle called me aside, when he came to take us off. He said, "Your mother doesn't know how to read."
>
> I said, "That's all right."
>
> For the reading you faced what they called commissioners, like judges on a bench. I was surrounded by my aunt and uncle and another uncle who's a pharmacist—my mother was in the center. They said she would have to take a test of reading. So one man said, "She can't speak English."
>
> Another man said, "We know that. We will give her a siddur." You know what a siddur is? It's a Jewish book. The night they said this, I knew that she couldn't do that and we would be in trouble.
>
> Well, they opened up a siddur. There was a certain passage they had you read. I looked at it and I saw right away what it was. I quickly studied it—I knew the whole paragraph. Then I got underneath the two of them there—I was very small—and I told her the words in Yiddish very

There are many stories about immigrants' names being changed or "Americanized" on Ellis Island. Historian Edward Oxford sheds some light on the subject in his fascinating article published in *American History Illustrated*.

"Scores of people who passed through Ellis Island later contended that during processing their names were changed or simplified. Although such acts have never been officially documented, stories of people receiving new names as they stood before the inspectors' desks are a revered part of America's oral history tradition.

An immigrant bearing the name Honnes Gardashian upon his arrival at Ellis Island left with the name Joe Arness. An Irish woman surnamed McGeoghegan somehow became McGaffighan. A man named Mastroianni emerged as Mister Yanni.

One Russian Jew had been told that some people changed their own names at Ellis Island. When he arrived, he asked a clerk to suggest a good name for use in America. 'Rockefeller,' the clerk advised. During his four-hour wait for an interview, the newcomer tried to remember how to say this odd name. When an inspector finally asked the Russian his name, the man sputtered, 'Shoyn feggessen!'—Yiddish for 'I have already forgotten!' The inspector wrote "Sean Fergusson" on the fellow's landing card, and a dazed new American-to-be wondered long and hard about his new name."

softly. I had memorized the lines and I said them quietly and she said them louder so the commissioner could hear it. She looked at it and it sounded as if she was reading it but I was doing the talking underneath. I was Charlie McCarthy![16]

How Names Were Changed

It has long been assumed that immigration inspectors "Americanized" or arbitrarily changed immigrants' names. This was not usually the case. Every effort was made to properly record the foreign names but miscommunication or mispronunciation of the names often resulted in changed spellings. The nervous and frightened immigrant did not wish to correct the inspector and simply agreed to whatever pronunciation the inspector made. Some immigrants even wanted a more American sounding name and chose one themselves—a new name to begin a new life.

"Entitled to Land"

Once the inspector entered the immigrant's name in the registry book and, in the words of the law, determined that the immigrant was "clearly and beyond a doubt entitled to land,"[17] the new arrival was issued a landing card. Statistics showed that three of every nine people issued a landing card were destined for New York City; the other six were bound for cities across the United States, probably to join family members already in residence.

The Staircase of Separation

At the end of the Great Hall was the Staircase of Separation. After questioning, all immigrants descended that staircase. At the bottom of the stairs, a turn to the right led to the railroad ticket office where tickets could be purchased for transport on the mainland; a turn to the left led to the ferry to Manhattan; straight ahead led to the dreaded detention rooms.

After descending, immigrants preparing to leave the island collected any baggage that had been checked and made their way to the money exchange to convert their lire, marks, francs, pounds, or rubles to dollars. Although convenient, the exchange rate offered was less than that at the banks on the mainland.

Employees helped those with railroad tickets determine how to reach their final destination. Those needing to purchase tickets crowded into the railroad ticket line. Many immigrants hoping to join family members had only sketchy ideas of where their relatives lived in this new country, and directions that had been given to them were incomplete. It was a challenge for railroad officials to decipher the addresses immigrants had scrawled

If immigrants were not granted railroad tickets or a spot on the ferry, they were held in detention rooms (pictured), which meant that their stay on Ellis Island continued.

on their baggage tags: "Detrayamis" (Detroit), "Linkinbra" (Lincoln, Nebraska), "Deas Moyness Youa" (Des Moines, Iowa), "Szckenevno Pillsburs" (Second Avenue, Pittsburgh)—or, simply, "Main Street."[18]

A food stand offered box lunches consisting of a sandwich, fruit, and a piece of pie for fifty cents to a dollar, much less expensive than food offered on the train. There was also a telegraph office available for those who needed to send messages to friends or relatives.

Immigrants waited in one more line to obtain a spot on the barges that would take them to the railway yard or on the Ellis Island ferry. The ferry was a double-decked 160-foot-long boat with the capacity for one thousand passengers. Between 1904 and 1954, when the ferry made her last run, she logged over a million miles shuttling immigrants to Manhattan.

With tickets in hand, ready to leave the building, the immigrants made their final walk down a hallway towards the door marked "Push, to New York." Once past that door, the immigrants knew they had earned their chance to make a life in America. Edward Corsi, an Ellis Island commissioner, once wrote of these hopeful people: "They were convinced . . . that America had enough and more for all who wished to come. It was only a question of being desired by the strong and wealthy country, of being worthy to be admitted."[19]

Ellis Island granted entry to more than 12 million people persuaded to leave everything behind to pursue their dreams in the United States.

Those Who Were Detained

The most frightening outcome an immigrant faced on Ellis Island was detainment or deportation. Many deportees had no homes to return to, having sold everything they owned to afford the passage to America. Detainees were obliged to live in crowded conditions in dormitories or, if recovering from an illness, confined in the hospital on the island.

The detainees generally fell into one of four categories: those detained for medical reasons, those briefly delayed for questioning, those waiting for a hearing by the Board of Special Inquiry, and those who appeared unable to make a living and were designated likely to become public charges. The latter group was most likely to be deported.

The Board of Special Inquiry

Twenty of every hundred immigrants went before the Board of Special Inquiry hoping inspectors' negative decisions would be overturned, and indeed, this was often the outcome. Only 2 percent of all immigrants were deported. The immigrants waiting for the chance to have their case heard before the Board of Special Inquiry had a variety of problems. Actually three boards (increased to

A detention pen on Ellis Island.

The commissioner of Ellis Island during the depression, Edward Corsi, bitterly recalls his opinion of deportation in Ann Novotny's book *Strangers at the Door.*

"Our deportation laws are inexorable and in many cases inhuman, particularly as they apply to men and women of honest behavior whose only crime is that they dared to enter the promised land without conforming to law. I have seen hundreds of such persons forced back to the countries they came from, penniless, and at times without coats on their backs. I have seen families separated, never to be united—mothers torn from their children, husbands from their wives, and no one in the United States, not even the President himself, able to prevent it."

tion), immigrants in violation of the contract labor law, and those determined likely to become a public charge who claimed they had relatives willing to take care of them, among other issues. Some Board of Special Inquiry rulings involved unusual cases, such as that of Mary Johnson, recounted by historian Mary Shapiro:

Mary . . . dressed in men's clothing and sporting a mustache, arrived at Ellis Island from Canada under the name Frank Woodhull. The truth was discovered in the inspection line. She was held for a hearing before a Board of Special Inquiry, during which she explained that as a woman she had limited opportunities: "Men can work at many unskilled callings, but to a woman only a few are open and they are grinding, death-dealing kinds of work. Well, for me, I prefer to live a life of independence and freedom." The board decided that Mary Johnson had a valid point. She was admitted and allowed to proceed to her destination, New Orleans.[20]

Bureaucratic Decision Making

The Board of Special Inquiry was appointed by the commissioner of immigration. The government inspectors were assisted by an interpreter and a stenographer was present to record the proceedings. The immigrants spoke directly to the board with no lawyer present. In case of an unfavorable ruling, an immigrant could appeal the decision to officials in charge of immigration in Washington, D.C. An immigrant could wait for weeks. A final decision on his or her appeal might take weeks or even months, and a detainee remained on the island during that time.

four during the peak seasons of spring, summer, and early fall due to a backlog of cases) were continually in session, deciding fifty to one hundred cases a day.

The board formed a court that consisted of three government inspectors who considered an immigrant's admission or exclusion. These cases varied widely; many were simply due to bureaucratic mixups that occurred when the immigrant boarded ship: an immigrant's history was not in agreement with what the inspectors had on file, or a name was incorrect, or an incorrect name was listed as sponsor of the immigrant. Cases often involved medical certification disputes (those who felt their particular medical condition was not severe enough to warrant deporta-

If requested by the immigrant, friends or relatives could come and testify on his or her behalf but were not required to do so. An early 1900s "Notice to Call on Behalf of a Detained Alien" included the name and ship of the alien and stated: "This alien refers to you. If you desire to call on his or her behalf, you may do so. Ferryboat leaves Barge Office (Battery Park), every half hour, on the hour. You are not required to pay anything to anyone in connection with this matter."[21]

Immigrants waiting for their case to be heard were not allowed to confer with their friends or relatives prior to the hearing.

Separate Cages

Those detained for medical treatment or on suspicion of mental illness were confined in caged rooms separate from the other immigrants. An interpreter who worked with the inspectors recalled,

The Kissing Post

In Edward Corsi's *In The Shadow of Liberty,* interpreter Frank Martocci recalls the great joy he witnessed at the Kissing Post, where relatives met detained immigrants once they were granted permission to leave the island.

"Incidentally, as you may have heard, there is a post at Ellis Island which through long usage has come to earn the name of 'The Kissing Post.' It is probably the spot of greatest interest on the Island, and if the immigrants recall it afterward it is always, I am sure, with fondness. For myself, I found it a real joy to watch some of the tender scenes that took place there.

There was a line of desks where the inspectors stood with their backs towards the windows and facing the wall. Further back, behind a partition, the witnesses waited outside for the detained aliens. As the aliens were brought out, the witnesses were brought in to be examined as to their rights of claim, If the inspector found no hitch, they were allowed to join each other. This, because of the arrangement of the partitions, usually took place at 'The Kissing Post,' where friends, sweethearts, husbands and wives, parents and children would embrace and kiss and shed tears for pure joy."

The Kissing Post is often remembered with fondness by immigrants who were granted permission to leave the island.

Detainment for most immigrants meant being caged up like animals.

They were lined up—a motley crowd in colorful costumes. . . . The alien was set aside in a cage apart from the rest, for all the world like a segregated animal, and his coat lapel or shirt marked with colored chalk, the color indicating why he had been isolated.[22]

Mental Examinations

One "medical" reason for detainment was to determine an immigrant's mental health, as U.S. immigration law at that time excluded the mentally retarded. Immigrants with questionable mental abilities were given special examinations to determine competence and sanity. These examinations were conducted with an interpreter aiding the immigrant to understand the testing procedures. Various types of tests were given to determine an immigrant's intelligence.

Early on, these mental tests were not tests at all; a physician merely spoke with an immigrant using an interpreter. Even simple questions and answers became difficult to conduct when the language barrier and foreign pride was factored in. For example, one test question asked: "Would you wash stairs from the top down or the bottom up?" One immigrant later reported that she replied: "I didn't come to America to wash stairs."[23]

Inspector Philip Cowan recounted his exchange with an Irish immigrant while trying to determine his skill in arithmetic:

"Pat, if I gave you two dogs and my friend gave you one, how many would you have?" "Four, sir," says Pat. "Did you ever go to school, Pat?" "Yes indeed, sir." "Now, Pat, if you had an apple and I gave you one, how many would you have?" "Two, sir." "And if my friend gave you one, how many would you have?" "Three, sir." Then repeating the original question, the answer was again, "Four, sir." "Why, Pat, how is that?" "Why, sir, I've got a dog at home meself."[24]

Psychotesting

In an attempt to improve this process, "psychotesting" was developed by assistant surgeon Howard A. Knox and adopted for use on the island in 1913. This method of testing was considered more reliable because it did not rely on language. The immigrant was asked to match selected designs of faces, leaves, and other common objects, or to fit wooden pegs into properly shaped holes on a board. Other simple tests involved choosing the happy (or sad) face from a series drawn on a chart, putting a simple wooden puzzle together, or describing an activity taking place in a particular picture.

Although this type of testing was an improvement, it was still common for an immigrant to give an incorrect answer. For example, when shown a picture of a boy burying his deceased pet rabbit, one immigrant believed the boy had been hunting for his supper. Yet individual doctors usually were able to account for these discrepancies. An immigrant had to fail the mental examinations three times before he was certified as mentally impaired and therefore subject to deportation.

Fiorello La Guardia, an Italian immigrant who later rose to prominence as a mayor of New York City, worked as an interpreter on Ellis Island. His sad memories of deported immigrants affected him for the rest of his life. He felt that many deportations due to mental health were unjustified and that the blame was to be laid in part on the doctors:

I felt then, and I feel the same today, that over fifty per cent of the deportations for alleged mental disease were unjustified. Many of those classified as mental cases

Italian immigrant Fiorello La Guardia became mayor of New York City after working as an interpreter on Ellis Island.

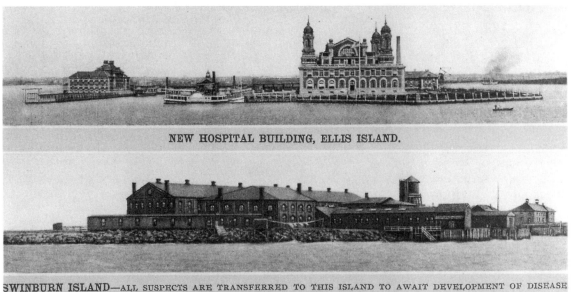

NEW HOSPITAL BUILDING, ELLIS ISLAND.

SWINBURN ISLAND—ALL SUSPECTS ARE TRANSFERRED TO THIS ISLAND TO AWAIT DEVELOPMENT OF DISEASE

SLAND—WHERE EMIGRANTS ARE SENT WHEN AFFLICTED WITH CONTAGIOUS DISEASES. THE LAST BUILDING I GROUND IS THE CREMATORY.

To accommodate the flood of patients, Ellis Island's medical facilities were expanded to include a contagious disease hospital and psychiatric ward.

were so classified because of ignorance on the part of the immigrants or the doctors and the inability of the doctors to understand the particular immigrants norm, or standard.[25]

Hospital Facilities

By far the greatest number of detentions on Ellis Island were due to disease. Large numbers of immigrants needed to be admitted to the hospital for either observation or treat-ment. Prior to the turn of the century, patients would be transferred to hospitals on the mainland. In 1902, however, the island was equipped with its own 125-bed hospital, built on a separate island known as Island No. 2, which had been constructed from landfill and was connected to the main island by a walkway. A surgeons' house was also built on this Island No. 2 for use by the doctors who often worked long hours and remained overnight.

The new hospital proved to be too small to accommodate the flood of patients, and many were still transferred to the mainland for treatment. Within nine years the hospital facilities were expanded twice, bringing the number of beds to 275. A contagious disease hospital was also opened in 1911 on newly constructed Island No. 3 (also built on land-fill) which provided an additional 450 beds. In this hospital was a separate locked psychiatric ward, Ward 13. During the peak years of immigration from 1905 to 1914, fifteen different medical buildings boasting state-of-the-art technology, were scattered on the islands.

No Medical Needs Are Neglected

The Ellis Island Committee, a group of men and women who reported on conditions at the island and the welfare of immigrants, declared in 1933 that the medical care was exemplary. This is consistent with opinions expressed by staff workers and patients since the hospital's beginning:

> In the opinion of the Committee, the character of medical care in the diagnostic treatment and administrative disposition of alien patients is at present of a high and creditable quality, equal to the best obtainable in modern general hospitals. In no essential respect is the social or technical medical need of the alien patient neglected. The best that modern medical science has to offer for American citizens who are charges of the U.S. Public Health Service in the hospitals operated solely in the interests of such patients is available and effectively used for aliens referred for diagnosis or treatment. The Committee wishes to express its entire confidence in the adequacy of medical care provided for aliens on Ellis Island and to recognize in this formal manner the high quality of professional and administrative service provided by the present commissioned personnel of the U.S. Public Health Service and their medical associates among contract surgeons and consultants.[26]

The distance between the islands as well as the isolation of various wards was intended to help control the spread of contagious diseases such as tuberculosis, smallpox, scarlet fever, and diphtheria. Several buildings were designated for measles patients. A section of the contagious disease hospital served children suffering from ailments such as whooping cough often contracted during the long ocean voyage. It was always distressing for immigrants when a family member was taken away for treatment. The remaining family members had to wait out the duration of the stay in crowded detention rooms with scant reports on the condition of loved ones. Although some accounts indicate patients saw their families regularly, more often than not family members were allowed few visits. In many instances, fear and frustration made the experience nearly unendurable for both the patient and the relatives. Despite the presence of interpreters, misunderstandings were common and hysteria set in easily. M. Gertrude Slaughter, an examining physician at the island in the early 1920s, recalls an incident that turned violent:

> It was in connection with the hospital that I saw one of the instances in which the attendants were the recipients of blows. Scarlet fever had developed in the child of an immigrant after the ship had passed quarantine. The parents were well and were directed to the first island, while the orderlies came with a stretcher to take

A Child Hospitalized

Angelina Palmiero, an Italian girl who came to America in 1923 at age ten, recalls her frightening and lonely hospitalization on Ellis Island in Peter Coan's book *Ellis Island Interviews*.

"When we got to Ellis Island, I went one way and my family went another. I don't know what happened to them. They brought me to the hospital. I was there for twenty-three days.

My sister, with my father and mother, went to Pennsylvania. My father had to pay a $250 bond that he would return to get me.

I wanted my mother. I was crying when they got me. There were two men that brought me into the hospital. I was kicking and screaming and after a while I got tired, and they put me in there with this girl who was older than I was. She must have been about thirteen, fourteen. 'Me Jew,' she said. She didn't speak Italian. I remember we got a kick out of the sliced bread in the morning when they brought us breakfast, and we would talk with our hands, and try to make each other understand. She only stayed about a week with me, because then I was left alone in there.

Nobody told me anything. Nobody explained, nobody said a word to me for twenty-three days. Just the nurse that came in and took my temperature. She gave me medicine. That's all I saw was the nurses. At night I use to pick up the gate. There was a gate that came down, and you pick it up. I would pick up the gate and walk to the end and go to the water and see the boats and the Statue of Liberty and the Staten Island Ferry. . . .

Then my mother got a telegram to come and get me. I remember standing in front of the judge by myself in the big hall. I was ten years old. There were thousands and thousands of people in there. I remember him sitting up high. 'All right, you sit there,' he said. And I sat there. . . . My father had to find me amongst all those people, but I knew him after having seen him from the ship. I knew he had grey hair. He was only thirty-three years old. There was nobody there with grey hair at the time who looked thirty-three years old. So I knew that it was him."

the child to the contagious ward. Immediately the mother attacked the attendants, beating and scratching them, and then tried to throw herself in the bay because she thought her child was being taken from her forever. Another attendant then had to hold the mother gently but firmly until an interpreter could be found who spoke her language; he explained the situation thoroughly, and peace was restored.[27]

Marge Glasgow, an immigrant who traveled alone to America from Scotland at the age of fifteen, remembers how terrified she was when doctors at Ellis Island determined she was to be admitted to the hospital:

I remember the Great Hall, and the desks there with men. I don't know if they were doctors, judges or what, questioning the people, you know. And that's when I was very scared, to be all alone in that big building being questioned. So I was really crying hysterically and sobbing so hard that the doctor came to me. They had doctors there examining everybody, and he put his arms around me and said, "Please, please, don't cry so hard. We're trying to help you. We only want to help you. We won't hurt you. We're helping you." And I said, "Perhaps the people didn't come to get me." And he said, "No, that's not the reason." He said, "You have something in your eyes that we have to test [trachoma], and it will take ten days to test. It might be a disease. But we are also investigating other people. You'll be taken care of. Everything will be fine."

So I sort of calmed down, and then a nurse came, and she took me. I was in the hospital there. She said, "Come with me." I was still a kid, fifteen. I followed her on her rounds, and she was very kind to me. She consoled me so much that I felt better. Then she put me to bed in a room next to her.[28]

"I Couldn't Hate It"

Many children who were admitted to the hospitals viewed the experience as a grand adventure and have happy memories of the kindnesses shown to them by health care

Such pastimes as playing ball, tennis, and going to movies proved fond memories for some immigrants.

employees. Elizabeth Martin, a Hungarian immigrant admitted for measles contracted on the island, fondly remembers the nurses who cared for her:

> The nurses were there. "Ladies in White" we used to call them. They were very nice. I mean, they talked to the children. They stroked their hair. And they touched their cheeks, and held our hands. When they gave us our milk, sometimes, maybe if there was a pretty child, some nurses would kiss the child on the cheek. They were really very nice.[29]

John Titone, a nine-year-old from Sicily, enjoyed many different activities while detained in the hospital:

> Some people hate Ellis Island. I couldn't hate it. Even though they kept me there, I wasn't mistreated. We could play outside. We'd play ball, play tennis, and the food was good. The library was good. Once a week, you'd go to the movies. Who could go to the movies once a week in Sicily, you know?[30]

"I Learned How to Speak English Very Quickly"

Many detainees proudly recall learning to speak English during their long hospital stays. Alvin Garrett, who came to America with his family in 1929, describes the process as a pleasant interlude in an interview with his sister Lois:

> LOIS: Then, when we had to be detained, it was like a shock. They examined us on the boat and that's when they found Alvin had a ringworm on his head, and that's

The Explosion That Shook Ellis Island

During World War I, in the early morning hours of July 30, 1917, German saboteurs set off an explosion on Black Tom Island (used for munitions storage) located only a few hundred yards from Ellis Island. The enormous impact blew out windows in Manhattan and caused $400,000 in damage to Ellis Island itself. No lives were lost and the 652 terrified people present on the island at the time were safely evacuated. In Ann Novotny's book *Strangers at the Door* a doctor recalls the reactions of the insane patients in Ward 13, the only ones who enjoyed the spectacle:

> As the five-inch shells flared over the Island like skyrockets, the poor demented creatures clapped their hands and cheered, laughed and sang and cried, thinking it was a show which had been arranged for their particular amusement.

why Papa couldn't take us directly from the boat home, and we were transported to Ellis Island.

ALVIN: The ringworm was considered very contagious at that time. Why they kept the rest of the family there six weeks I don't know. But they kept me at the hospital on Ellis Island.

LOIS: I remember going to see you in the hospital.

ALVIN: They came to see me every day. And the nurses were crazy about me because I was a . . .

LOIS: . . . Cute little boy. I remember being in the hospital running up and down the wards, and everybody being good to me. I had a wonderful time. From the nurses, I learned how to speak English very quickly. By the time we left there, Alvin was speaking like a native American.

ALVIN: When I left Ellis Island people couldn't believe that I wasn't born American. . . . The bad part was they took off my hair by electrolysis, and they told my mother, "Your son will never have hair again." And to this day I have a bald spot. My hair has been the same way for sixty years. It hasn't changed.[31]

Deaths and Births

Ellis Island records show that many who fell ill during their long detention, or who were admitted to one of the hospitals, did not recover. Over thirty-five hundred persons (four-teen hundred of whom were children) died on the island. Their stories are heartbreaking. Martha Strahm lost her two-year-old son in 1920:

> Walter took sick and was admitted to the hospital. He was there six weeks and died on February 9, 1921. We were confined on Ellis Island those six weeks. Our days were very long days and only one of us could go visit our sick boy for five minutes once a week. . . . Our boy died at ten min-utes after 11:00 P.M. . . . After all these years the picture in my mind is so clear when they took him down the hall wrapped in a sheet.[32]

There were also many moments of happi-ness when babies were born on the island. Some 355 births took place on Ellis Island. These new arrivals, born to immigrant par-ents, were automatically American citizens.

3 | Daily Life on the Island

In order to process arriving immigrants and to care for the many who were detained, Ellis Island operated like a small city. One constant, especially during the late 1800s that continued well into the following century, was overcrowding. There was neither sufficient space nor sufficient facilities. Available beds were in short supply as were baths and toilets. Dormitories and detention rooms were vermin infested and there was initially little space provided for recreation.

Barbara Barondess, who arrived on the island from Russia in 1921, recalls the paradox of the grandeur of the building and the dismal living conditions she encountered:

> I used to go and look at this beautiful, fantastic building that, as we were arriving, looked like a palace and inside looked like a bare jail. . . .
>
> You had to wait in line to get the food. You had to wait in line to get a blan-

Immigrants remember being herded like cattle as they winded through the metal railings to be processed.

ket. . . . They weren't unkind, but they had so many people to take care of.[33]

Understandably, many of the detained immigrants grew angry and frustrated. Greta Wagner, a young German woman traveling alone, arrived on the island in 1923 and found the experience embittering. She did not have any money and was saved from deportation by a Catholic charity who agreed to give her room and board until she found a job and was able to support herself. Her words reflect her dislike for Ellis Island:

We were shipped first to Ellis Island and that was not very pleasant. It was rough, very rough. Years ago, they called it a cattle farm. Oh, it was just like a barn. Millions of people standing around with the bundles. You were with a big herd. And they fed us with a wagon full of that cattle food. They slapped it on the plates.

You were just like a number. Over 5,000 a day were arriving from all over—Russia, Romania, Poland, from Germany, from France, and naturally I couldn't speak one word of English. . . . I was detained for two weeks. I talked with the directors every day but I couldn't explain anything. But they wouldn't let me go. They wanted to send me back to Germany. . . . Nobody got off Ellis Island unless they were called for by someone who would stand good for them. Somebody had to come up and sign.[34]

Her assessment of the situation was close to the mark. Dormitories and dayrooms were continually packed with a throng of people speaking innumerable languages, unable to make sense of their situation. As one inspector remembers, "Those days we averaged about two thousand [detained every night]. In

the detention room there were never less than nine hundred. It was an endless affair, like filling a trough at one end and emptying it at the other."[35]

Detention Rooms

Detention quarters were referred to as "pens." Meant for short-term use, the dirty, large, wire cells were filled beyond capacity with immigrants waiting to hear their fate or waiting for a family member recovering in the hospital. The cells were designed to accommodate six hundred people but as many as nine hundred to seventeen hundred immigrants were crushed together within their wire walls. Immigrants being detained were deloused and their clothing fumigated to combat lice. "They put my mother and me in the showerroom," recounted a woman who had been detained with her parents for a week. "They hosed us down. I cried. I yelled that they were burning me with the hot water. It was bitter tears I shed."[36] The rooms were also scrubbed daily yet they were still infested with vermin.

The Dormitories

Nowhere on the island were conditions worse than in the overcrowded dormitories. The main building had several dormitory rooms, the largest two located along the balcony of the Great Hall. The rooms were quickly filled to capacity and surplus detainees were then sent to sleep in temporary wooden sheds constructed behind the main building. In 1910 the wooden sheds were replaced by a brick facility which served as a baggage and dormitory building.

The beds in the dormitories had no mattresses and merely consisted of wire mesh or canvas stretched across a frame. These were stacked in triple-tier bunks spaced two feet apart and surrounded by a wire mesh enclosure. Immigrants were issued two blan-

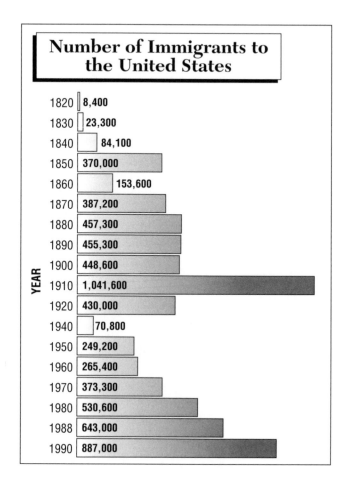

Number of Immigrants to the United States

YEAR	Number
1820	8,400
1830	23,300
1840	84,100
1850	370,000
1860	153,600
1870	387,200
1880	457,300
1890	455,300
1900	448,600
1910	1,041,600
1920	430,000
1940	70,800
1950	249,200
1960	265,400
1970	373,300
1980	530,600
1988	643,000
1990	887,000

Although many immigrants detested their time on Ellis Island, a Frenchwoman expressed her appreciation at the treatment she received there in the mid-1920s in a letter to Commissioner Curran, as quoted in Thomas Pitkin's *Keepers of the Gate*.

"GENTLEMEN:
After a life of travel, and study, knowing five languages, it might have been supposed that I had seen everything worthy of interest, yet I had lately an excellent opportunity to study an institution unique in the world, and extremely interesting. I mean Ellis Island.

The construction is vast and imposing tho often crowded by the immense quantity of emigrants, whose absolute ignorance prevents many to appreciate that the short detention is not only imposed for the security of United States, but for their own welfare.

The ladies and gentleman in charge of the immigrants have inexhaustible patience and kindness. The large admittion hall is (in the evening) used as a concert room (once a week) and cinema once also. Sundays a Catholic, a Protestant and Jewish services are held so any creed can be followed. All this is free. Above, all around the hall, is a balcony. This have white tile walls and floors, porcelaine lavabos and baths. There are two hospital, a kindergarten, medical attendance, all free as well as board logging, entertainment, etc. etc. Interrogation rooms, etc., are on the ground floor. Besides breakfast (coffee, eggs, bread, butter, jam) (lunch—meat, vegetables, cheese, tea) dinner (soup, meat, etc.) there are (morning, afternoon, evening) three distributions of the best of sweet fresh milk and crackers. Many days thirty of those enormous cans are needed (they contain fifty gallons each, I was told). Six hundred and fifty employees are daily in attendance. Eighteen languages are interpreted. From morning till night colored men and women clean incessantly. Towels are changed daily. Sheets three times a week.

I leave to a competent man to estimate of the daily expense of such an establishment, and I should thank heartily an expert to compare Ellis Island to anything of the same sort, any other nation in the wide world has to offer.

This statement is not solicited, but if it can make emigrants understand and appreciate what U.S. does for them, you are welcome to publish it (in any and all of the eighteen languages understood at Ellis Island).

Thanking you for all passed favors, I remain,
        Gratefully yours,
        F. M. LaLande"

kets, one to sleep on and one for a cover. The immigrants often refused to use them as the blankets were usually infested with lice.

Traditional Enemies

The immigrants' indignation over unsanitary and crowded conditions was intensified when they were forced to share intolerably close quarters with people who, in the old country, were considered enemies. Such was the situation for a Slovenian immigrant, Louis Adamic, during his detention in 1913:

The first night in America I spent, with hundreds of other recently arrived immigrants, in an immense hall with tiers of narrow iron-and-canvas bunks, four deep. . . . The bunk immediately beneath mine was occupied by a Turk. . . . I thought how curious it was that I should be spending a night in such proximity to a Turk, for Turks were traditional enemies of Balkan peoples, including my own nation. For centuries Turks had forayed into Slovenian territory. Now here I was, trying to sleep directly above a Turk, with only a sheet of canvas between us.[37]

Feeding the Hungry

The number of people on staff at Ellis Island averaged between 500 and 850, including immigration officers, clerks, interpreters, guards, matrons, gatekeepers, watchmen, cooks, engineers, firemen, painters, gardeners, doctors, nurses, and orderlies.

This staff had to learn to accommodate a huge number of cultures and customs. This problem presented itself most persistently in

Immigrants having lunch on Ellis Island.

the dining room. Seating twelve hundred, the dining room was furnished with large rectangular tables lined on each side with long wooden benches. Men and boys sat together at the front of the room while women and young children clustered together at tables in the back. Everyone hungered for familiar food and rarely got it. In fact, in the early days of Ellis Island the immigrants received barely enough food to subsist on.

In the early 1890s the dining room was operated by a private company under contract to the U.S. Immigration Service. Steamship companies were required by law to provide meals to all immigrants being detained and were billed accordingly to cover the costs of doing so. Early food concessions were corrupt, however, taking money and providing inadequate and often inedible meals. It was even rumored that inspectors detained immigrants longer than necessary just to increase the number of meals served, for which they skimmed a share of the funds paid by the shipping companies.

Immigrants also experienced unfair treatment and even abuse. The *London Express* gave a chilling account of a typical meal experienced by reporters investigating the island in 1901:

We passed in a long line around the room. A man with filthy hands filled our hats or handkerchiefs with mouldy prunes. Another thrust two lumps of bread in our hands. Supervising the distribution was a foul mouthed Bowery tough, who danced upon the tables and poured forth upon us torrents of obscene blasphemous abuse. I saw him drag an old man, a long-bearded Polish Jew, past the barrel of prunes by the hair of his face. I saw him kick another immigrant, a German, on the head with a heavy boot.[38]

A 1902 report also revealed the deplorable conditions of the kitchens and dining room: "The kitchen methods and methods of serving food to the immigrants are filthy and unsanitary in every way."[39]

Dishonesty, Thievery, and Corruption

Filthy conditions in the dining room and poor fare were the least of the problems on the island. At the turn of the century a major scandal erupted over corruption and mistreatment of immigrants. Reporters and ordinary citizens were moved to investigate and uncovered numerous shocking facts. Edward Steiner, an immigrant who became a clergyman and teacher,

At the turn of the century, unsavory practices were common on Ellis Island. Edward Steiner, a minister who traveled in steerage to investigate matters for himself, comments on the problems he encountered in Pamela Reeves's book *Ellis Island: Gateway to the American Dream.*

"I knew that the money changers were 'crooked,' so I passed a 20 mark piece to one of them for exchange, and was cheated out of nearly 75 percent of my money. My change was largely composed of new pennies, whose brightness was well calculated to deceive any newcomer.

At another time I was approached by an inspector who, in a very friendly way, intimated that I might have difficulty in being permitted to land, and that money judiciously placed might accomplish something.

A Bohemian girl whose acquaintance I had made on the steamer came to me with tears in her eyes and told me that one of the inspectors had promised to pass her quickly, if she would promise to meet him at a certain hotel. In heartbroken tones she asked: 'Do I look like that?'"

made several transatlantic crossings to expose the worst of the corruption and scandal. He documented being robbed of nearly three-quarters of his money in unfair exchanges at the money exchange. He also reported instances of immigrants forced to work in the unsanitary kitchen, and that the dishes and dining room facilities were hardly ever cleaned. His reports revealed that the restaurant was being robbed by the employees and proprietor alike. He recorded that "roughness, cursing, intimidation and a mild form of blackmail"[40] were common on the island. Steiner also reported that inspectors accepted bribes to sign blank landing cards to be filled in by immigrants before inspecton. Some inspectors preyed on pretty girls, promising them passage in exchange for sexual favors. Immigration inspectors boarding the steamships in the quarantine areas would sell fake certificates of citizenship, then split the profits with ships' officers who looked the other way. Corrupt railroad agents on the island sold tickets at inflated prices by unnecessarily routing immigrants through several states on the way to their final destination.

Terence Powderly, commissioner of the Bureau of Immigration in Washington, appointed a commission to gather evidence of wrongdoing, and in June 1900, eleven Ellis Island employees were fired. Even these radical steps could not completely resolve corrupt practices.

President Roosevelt Steps In

Within a month of taking office in September 1901, Theodore Roosevelt began work on the situation at Ellis Island. His first step was to search for a reliable commissioner. The man he chose was William Williams, a wealthy Wall Street lawyer with some government experience. Williams served as commissioner from 1902 to 1905 and again from 1909 to 1913.

Williams immediately posted a notice in all public buildings on the island:

Immigrants must be treated with kindness and consideration. Any government official violating the terms of this notice will be recommended for dismissal from the service. Any other person doing so will be forthwith required to leave Ellis Island. It is earnestly requested that any violation hereof, or any instance of any kind of improper treatment of immigrants at Ellis Island, or before they leave the Barge Office, be promptly brought to the attention of the commissioner.[41]

Williams's Regime

This policy was strictly adhered to. One telegraph boy was caught giving an immigrant counterfeit coins and was immediately jailed on charges filed by Williams himself. Several drunken employees were fired and fines were levied on steamship companies with inaccurate manifests.

Within months of taking office Williams also terminated all contracts for food, baggage, and money exchange concessions found to have been cheating immigrants. These concessions had been run by politically powerful forces and Williams came under fire for his decision but President Roosevelt stood by him and the crooked concessions were terminated. When awarding the new contracts Williams made it clear that the first

Corruption and mistreatment of immigrants sparked Theodore Roosevelt to take action to better the conditions on Ellis Island.

Daily Life on the Island

consideration was to see the best interests of the immigrants served.

The replacement concessions company improved the immigrants' diet considerably. Simple but nourishing food was served, and extra snacks such as crackers and milk were allotted to women and children. A typical menu from 1906 reads:

BREAKFAST: coffee with milk and sugar, and bread and butter. Crackers and milk for women and children.

DINNER: Beef stew, boiled potatoes and rye bread. Smoked or pickled herring for Hebrews. Crackers and milk for women and children.

SUPPER: Baked beans, stewed prunes and rye bread, and tea with milk and sugar. Crackers and milk for women and children.[42]

By 1911, a kosher kitchen was added for the benefit of the many Jewish immigrants who refused to eat food not prepared according to Jewish law.

Negative Reactions

Even with improvements, changes, and compromises, the problem of feeding such a varied group of people was never satisfactorily resolved. Commissioner Edward Coors remembers the reactions of various cultures to the food they were given:

At times there have been twenty-five or thirty races in detention at one time. The Italian cares nothing for the dried fish preferred by the Scandinavian, and

"The Passing of a Great Race"

American anthropologist Madison Grant, author of *The Passing of a Great Race* (1916), echoed the anti-immigrant feelings of many Americans in his book. Wilton Tifft excerpts a powerful passage from Grant's work in his own book *Ellis Island*.

"These new immigrants were no longer exclusively members of the Nordic race as were the earlier ones who came of their own impulse to improve their social conditions. The transportation lines advertised America as a land flowing with milk and honey and the European government took the opportunity to unload upon careless, wealthy and hospitable America the sweepings of their jails and asylums. . . . The new immigration . . . contained a large and increasing

number of the weak, the broken and the mentally crippled of all races drawn from the lowest stratum of the Mediterranean basin and the Balkans, together with hoards of the wretched, submerged populations of the Polish ghettos. Our jails, insane asylums, and alms-houses are filled with this human flotsam. . . .

These immigrants adopt the language of the native American, they wear his clothes, they steal his name and they are beginning to take his women, but they seldom adopt his religion or understand his ideals, and while he is being elbowed out of his own home the American looks calmly abroad and urges on others the suicidal ethics which are exterminating his own race."

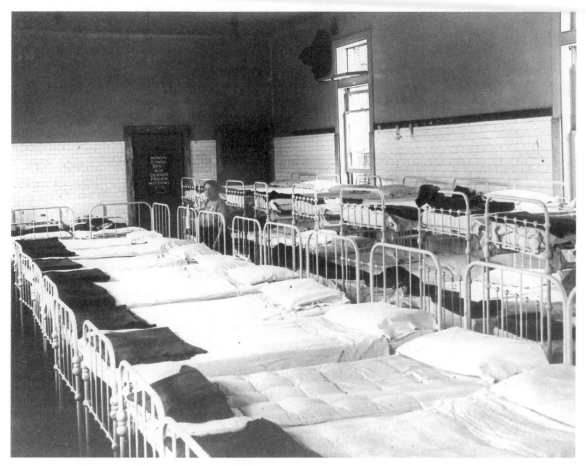

Once William Williams took over as commissioner, he made improvements to the unsanitary conditions of the dormitories.

the Scandinavian has no use for spaghetti. The Greek wants his food sweetened, and no one can make tea for an Englishman. The basis of all Asiatic and Malay food is rice, which they will mix with almost anything. The Chinese take to other foods but want rice in place of bread. The Mohammed's will eat no food across which the shadow of an infidel has fallen. And in big years it has been Superintendent Baker's problem to serve nine thousand meals per day, trying to please all.[43]

Williams also saw that the unsanitary conditions in the dormitory and detention rooms were improved. Nevertheless, overcrowding remained a problem. Although outright abuse was curtailed, immigrants still felt bewildered and ignored, as Paul Knaplund, a Norwegian immigrant, recalls:

"The newcomers were pushed around a good deal," but felt this could be due to the fact that they were "so numerous and unfamiliar with the language of the officials." [Knaplund] "had the

The Plight of a Woman Alone

Edward Corsi, a former commissioner of Ellis Island, describes the particular problems of women coming to America alone. His comments, documented in Virginia Yans-McLaughlin's book *Ellis Island and the Peopling of America*, reflect the heartbreak these brave women faced.

"There were times, of course, when all our efforts to locate immediate relatives failed. Sometimes a married woman had come to join her husband, or a young woman to marry her fiancé, and the man could not be located. Perhaps he had died, or moved, or the correspondence hadn't reached him— who knows? In any event, the results were tragic indeed, as I well know from personal experience. There was no way of soothing these heartbroken women who had traveled thousands and thousands of miles, endured suffering and humiliation, and who had uprooted their lives only to find their hopes shattered at the end of the long voyage. These, I think, are the saddest of all immigration cases.

Sometimes these women were placed in the care of a social agency which agreed to be responsible to the Commissioner [of Immigration], caring for them or placing them in some appropriate occupation. But if everything possible had been done, and the missing husband or fiancé still could not be traced, the poor alien, despite all her tears, had to be returned to her native country."

feeling that he was not being treated as a human being but as a commodity to be processed."[44]

In defense of the Williams regime, the editors of *Leslie's Weekly* of August 7, 1902, praised the improvements: "The aliens are now treated in the main quite as considerately as would be crowds of like size and character in the heart of the city."[45]

Historian Thomas Pitkin concludes that Ellis Island was "probably run with as much consideration for the immigrant as its overwhelming problems and the frailty of human nature would permit."[46]

Williams's Personal Prejudices

The commissioner had indeed wrought a small miracle on Ellis Island, and acquired many enemies in doing so. And although he tolerated no abuse of any immigrant, his personal attitudes toward certain immigrant groups reflected widespread prejudices of the day. Williams believed that eastern and southern European immigrants were inferior to those coming from England, Germany, and Scandinavian countries. He favored stronger restrictions, and as a result, took it upon himself to exclude large numbers of immigrants who would have gained entry under previous commissioners. President Roosevelt initiated an investigation and appointed a special commission to look into Williams's administrative performance.

Roosevelt Visits the Island

Roosevelt (probably prompted by the unfavorable press coverage of the exclusions) made a surprise visit to the island on September 16, 1903. During the visit, Roosevelt "held an impromptu hearing in the case of a woman and her four children, who, bound about with official red tape, had been languishing in the detention pen for nearly two months and promptly set them free."[47]

Williams survived both the visit and the investigation. In fact, he received high praise for his supervisory and administrative practices.

"A Lack of Imagination"

Another man who worked diligently to improve conditions for the immigrants on Ellis Island was Frederic C. Howe, who served as commissioner from 1914 to 1919. One of his associates wrote of Howe that he "had the progressive idea that Government should be the best friend of the immigrant, until he became a citizen; that he should come to it for guidance and protection."[48]

Howe's comments on improving the examination rooms serve as good examples of his general attitude. He stated: "We want to take down the wire netting from around the examination rooms, which makes them feel like animals in a cage, and then we'll hang maps and pictures on the walls. The only thing that is lacking over here is imagination. No one ever seemed to try to imagine what a detained immigrant must be feeling."[49] These reforms were very controversial and unpopular with many citizens and politicians who did not want money spent to improve the lives of

With its wire fencing and metal bars, many immigrants on Ellis Island felt like prisoners.

immigrants who were unwelcome by a vast majority of Americans.

And while the immigrants enjoyed the benefits of the changes and were no longer robbed or overtly abused, they still hated being detained and deprived of true individual freedom. Gustav Glaser, a Danish immigrant detained in 1924, expressed his feelings of helplessness: "You didn't feel like you were free. They treated you like prisoners. I mean, why did they have to lock the door with a key and have a man standing outside watching? It's an island. Ellis Island is an island. We couldn't walk anywhere."[50]

Recreation and Daily Activity

Commissioner Howe permitted the immigrants to make use of the lawns for outdoor recreation. Families, previously separated, could meet for visits. A rooftop garden was also constructed with swings and a play area for children. Athletic games and exercise classes were organized. Rooms were made available for adults to hold meetings and socialize. Needlework and sewing classes were offered to the women with materials donated by local organizations. A free library was opened with donations of books and pam-

Improvements such as outdoor recreation, gardens, games, and play areas for children helped to ease detainment for some immigrants.

Musical groups performed free concerts for the entertainment of immigrants on Ellis Island.

phlets in numerous languages from the New York Public Library. Howe also arranged with the New York Board of Education for classes to be taught in English and other elementary subjects for the benefit of children detainees. Films were shown once or twice a week and musical groups gave free concerts.

Frank Martocci, an interpreter during this time, recalled how popular the concerts were during World War I when many Germans and other enemy aliens caught in the harbor at the start of the war were detained on the island with the immigrants. When war broke out, all Germans in ships in the harbor which had not been processed, including sailors on foreign ships and tourists, were detained as enemy aliens. "For persons being detained, these enemy aliens were treated royally. There were concerts on Sundays in the large detention room upstairs. Because many of these accidentally detained Germans did not pose a threat, they were treated well. Friends of the enemy aliens came in such numbers that three or four trips had to be made by the Island ferryboat."[51]

Marriages on the Island

Marriages were another ritual of daily life. Many of the female immigrants had been contracted by marriage brokers and matrimonial agencies to leave their homeland and marry U.S. immigrant citizens who wanted women of their own nationality. The women, known as "picture brides," sent photographs of themselves to prospective grooms, and if accepted, were sent for through agency channels. It was not uncommon for a bride to change her mind on arrival, but the women had no alternative. If they appealed to the Board of Special Inquiry and the board was satisfied the man was able to provide support, the couple was married on the island or the woman faced deportation. Sometimes, the bridegroom failed to show up to claim his bride or the bride fell in love with a fellow immigrant during the journey to America and chose to marry him instead, but in most instances the wedding proceeded as planned. Catholic priests were available for these ceremonies as well as Protestant clergymen and secular judges. Hundreds of marriages were performed, as Frank Martocci remembers:

> It seems to me now as I look back that in those days there were crying and laughing and singing all the time at Ellis Island. Very often brides came over to marry here, and of course we had to act as witnesses. I have no count, but I'm sure I must have helped at hundreds and hundreds of weddings of all nationalities and all types. The weddings were numberless until they dropped the policy of marrying them at the Island and brought them to City Hall in New York.[52]

Christmas Celebrations Remembered

Rita Bellmer, daughter of Martin Bellmer, who was chief of mail, files, and records at Ellis Island from 1919 until 1954, recalls Christmas celebrations she enjoyed as a child on Ellis Island in Peter Coan's *Ellis Island Interviews*.

"As a youngster I came over to Ellis Island quite frequently. I would come with my mother. At Christmastime, there was always a Christmas service. A member of the clergy conducted it, and it was for the participation of all the immigrants. They sang Christmas songs and carols, and they had a gigantic Christmas tree at the end of the Great Hall. The families of the employees were invited out.

It was fascinating. I didn't have any apprehension about the immigrants or about coming here. That was his job. There was no thought about differences of nationalities or any such thing. It was just taken for granted. It was exciting to take the ferry ride and to go where Daddy worked. His office was off a balcony. He did not wear a uniform but he had to carry his badge and his identification. I wasn't allowed to talk to the immigrants. Even at Christmas. I was upstairs where the offices were. The service was conducted downstairs, and I was upstairs on the balcony observing and singing along.

I had his name put on the Wall of Honor. I felt that my father had given so many years of service all of his working life on Ellis Island. And even though he did not come to this country as an immigrant, I felt that I wanted to have his name there as a kind of memorial to him. And then last October my son and his wife and youngster were here to visit, and they saw it, and they took a picture of my granddaughter with her finger on her great-granddaddy's name."

Holidays on the Island

Christmas, Passover, and other holidays were celebrated on Ellis Island, often organized by immigrant aid societies and religious organizations. Ukrainian Jewish immigrant Fannie Friedman remembers Passover 1921: "It was Passover and some Jewish people came. They said, 'How many Jewish people are here? We have a kosher meal for you.' And we came to the table. And there were people from the HIAS [Hebrew Immigrant Aid Society] who were attending to everything, telling everyone where to sit and serving and all that."[53]

Christmas was celebrated with a tall, decorated tree erected on the balcony overlooking the Great Hall. The children were treated to a visit from Santa Claus and were given gifts from the Ellis Island staff—cards, candy, oranges, or maybe a small toy. Special musical performances were arranged; on one Christmas Eve the great Enrico Caruso himself sang, a performance never forgotten by Helen Cohen of Poland: "Caruso! The real Caruso! He sang for us. His voice is still ringing in my ears! But then the loudspeaker called out our family's name. My cousin had come to take us out. We ran out quick—even on Caruso—to get out of Ellis Island."[54]

For the most part staff members and commissioners attempted to help preserve the dignity of the immigrants, offering food they would enjoy, and some entertainment and recreation to pass the long hours.

4 Immigrant Aid Societies

The history of the social organizations that were formed to provide aid to immigrants precedes the existence of the Ellis Island immigration station. The German Emigrant Society was formed in 1784, and in 1841, the Irish Emigrant Society was organized. Both groups helped immigrants of specified nationalities assimilate to life in the United States. With the huge influx of immigrants coming through Ellis Island, the societies' representatives began to go to the island itself to provide assistance, comfort, and even financial aid if necessary.

Over forty immigrant aid societies were represented at Ellis Island, with over one hundred workers holding passes giving them

Not only did social service organizations provide comfort to the flood of immigrants, they also acted as interpreters, helped locate luggage, and contacted the friends and families of detained immigrants.

free access to the detention rooms and hospitals. Many of these groups were provided with office space on the island. The two largest were the Hebrew Immigrant Aid Society (HIAS) and the Society for the Protection of Italian Immigrants. Other active and important groups included the YWCA, the Daughters of the American Revolution, the Salvation Army, the Red Cross, the Traveler's Aid Society, the American Tract Society, the Congregational Home Missionary Society, the Inner Mission Board of the Lutheran Church, the Italian Welfare League, the National Catholic Welfare Conference, the National Council of Jewish Women, the National Institute of Immigrant Welfare, the New York Bible Society, the New York Protestant Episcopal City Mission Society, and the Women's Christian Temperance Union, among others. Many of the groups were dedicated to helping all immigrants regardless of nationality.

Many Tasks to Accomplish

Much of their work involved dealing with the daily lives of the immigrants in detention. Religious counsel was provided to those in need or to those simply fearful of their situation and wishing for someone to talk to. The social workers also organized games, recreational events, concerts, and parties.

Representatives of social service groups also acted as interpreters when necessary, helped locate lost luggage, and assisted immigrants with contacting friends and relatives on the mainland. Social service workers also acted as advocates for the immigrants during hearings before the Board of Special Inquiry and assisted immigrants in making appeals.

These dedicated people distributed milk, crackers, and cookies to the children on a daily basis and often gave American clothing to the women from the secondhand closet maintained by donations. Their main goals were to provide assistance, protect immigrants' rights, and help newcomers assimilate to their new environment in any way they could.

Most of the social workers' deeds were appreciated by the frightened, homesick immigrants. Ludmila K. Foxlee, an Ellis Island social worker from 1920 to 1937, recalls her own experience:

> They tell us that we help lighten the burden of detention with our daily visits. . . . Above all this . . . they want our friendliness. . . . No one can speak the twenty-five-odd languages in which aliens speak who pass through Ellis Island, but by dividing the social work services on a language basis, almost all the people who need it get the friendly attention they crave.[55]

A Place to Work and a Place to Live

One of the most valuable services of these groups saved many immigrants from certain deportation, namely, finding work and lodging for the new arrivals and agreeing to take responsibility for their welfare. Many immigrant aid societies ran employment services, which enabled them to steer the immigrants to honest employers not likely to take advantage of them. Particularly in the case of an immigrant woman alone, these legitimate employment opportunities saved her from falling into the trap of prostitution. The social workers escorted their charges from the ferries, through Battery Park, and directly to the safety of their offices.

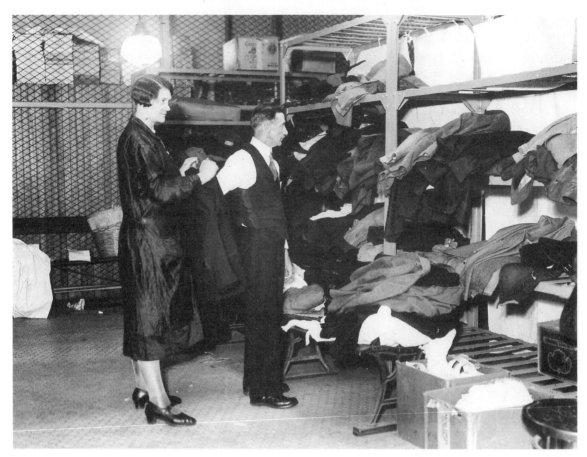

Social workers helped immigrants find work with honest employers, acted as advocates during hearings, and distributed food and clothing.

General Committee on Immigrant Aid

In 1918 the agencies working on Ellis Island banded together to form the General Committee on Immigrant Aid at Ellis Island. Representatives from each group, known as welfare workers, attended monthly meetings to discuss any problems encountered and to keep abreast of current legislation affecting immigrants. The group worked closely with the government and served as both a buffer

and a liaison between the government and the immigrants. It also served as a watchdog, monitoring conditions on the island and issuing reports of its findings. Happily, between the efforts of the social workers and of Ellis Island staff, conditions improved steadily through the years:

> In its contacts with the officials and personnel at Ellis Island, the Committee found a high average of competency and intelligence and generally a sympathetic handling of the alien. It was especially

impressed with the enlightened supervision under which the Island was administered and is convinced that only under such supervision and leadership can the best interests of the Immigration and Naturalization Service be achieved both in the faithful execution of our laws and in the just and humane treatment of the alien.[56]

Unstinted Praise

The amazing accomplishments of the immigration aid societies were not entirely overlooked. *Leslie's Weekly* praised the workers serving at Ellis Island:

One of the notable features of the care taken of the immigrants . . . is the attention paid to them by missionaries of several religious denominations and the agents of benevolent societies. . . . These people were continually on the watch for cases of need and distress, and had been the means of preventing injustice and affording succor in countless instances. The work they are doing, is of the kind that merits unstinted praise.[57]

Settlement Houses

Social workers were just as important to immigrants after their entry into the United States. Protective societies and settlement houses dedicated to helping immigrants adjust to their new surroundings and become productive citizens were established in large cities all over the country in the 1880s. Some, such as the German Lutheran Home for Immigrants in New York and the Lutheran Pil-

grim House, were affiliated with particular denominations or nationalities, but many helped all immigrants regardless of their background. Settlement houses adapted to local conditions and specific needs in various cities. The most well known settlement houses were Stanton Coit's Neighborhood Guild, established in 1886 in New York City; Lillian Wald's Henry Street Settlement, established in 1893 in New York City; South End House, established by Robert A. Woods in Boston in 1891; and Hull House, established by Jane Addams in Chicago in 1889.

These settlement houses provided services as varied as reading, writing, speech and English classes; cooking, hygiene, and home economics classes; and music and singing lessons. One of their most important functions was to serve as a center for social activity that brought neighbors together for parties, sewing circles, plays, and other performance art, and planned meetings for neighborhood improvement. Settlement houses were also after-school havens for children, who could safely receive help with their homework, play in the playground under supervision, or read from a selection of books in the library. Settlement houses also provided medical help when necessary and assisted immigrants in the naturalization process to become American citizens.

Social clubs sponsored by various organizations and settlement houses were also very important to immigrants offering them opportunities to mix with each other and with members of the community. Abraham Beame (Birnbaum) who came to this country as a baby in 1906, recalls how important his social club was to him as a young adult:

Part of the purpose of the settlement houses was to keep the kids off the

Social Welfare Work on the Island

The official Ellis Island website offers much interesting information about the history of Ellis Island. This excerpt from the commissioner's report (Reports of the Immigration Commission, vol. 37, p. 129) on Immigrant Homes and Immigrant Aid Societies describes their work.

Religious and philanthropic societies flocked to Ellis Island as missionaries selling Bibles, gospel tracts, and other literature.

"In order to afford such immigrants the opportunity of landing and also to help them and other aliens to avoid dangers that are likely to be encountered, certain philanthropic and religious societies have undertaken the work of assisting immigrants upon their arrival at the various large ports of this country. These societies, by special permission of the Government, send missionaries and representatives, the majority of whom are of the races they are employed to assist, to the immigrant stations and to the Government detention rooms for the purpose of aiding incoming immigrants in every necessary and proper way. In the furtherance of this object many of the societies establish homes where the immigrants may be temporarily lodged and cared for. . . .

Missionaries and representatives assist arriving immigrants in various ways. They write letters for them and help them to get into communication with their friends and relatives in this country; trace lost baggage; give religious consolation; escort immigrants to their destinations in the city without charge except for car fares or other necessary expenses; take the names and addresses of immigrants of specific races or religions who are going to points outside of the city and forward these lists to organizations of the same race or religion at the points of destination; distribute clothing, Bibles, gospel tracts, and other literature; sell Bibles and gospels (in 1907 the amount of these sales at one immigrant station was $1,013.97); investigate the cases of detained and excluded immigrants and the causes of such detentions or exclusion; appear before the boards of special inquiry in behalf of detained immigrants and give evidence secured from conversations with the immigrants or from other sources; reopen the cases of excluded immigrants by appealing from the decisions of the station authorities to the Department of Commerce and Labor; secure bonds for excluded immigrants; and have discharged in their care immigrants whose friends or relatives have failed to meet them on arrival, those whose friends and relatives are unable to satisfy the immigration authorities that they are proper persons to receive and care for the immigrants, those who are waiting for money to be forwarded in order that they may continue their journey, or those who are awaiting the recovery of a sick member of the family in the station hospital."

streets. It was the difference between becoming a rowdy and growing up to be a criminal, or becoming a good citizen. And there was a lot of rowdiness at that time. You had to be careful in those days. If you were Jewish and you walked into a non-Jewish area, you might have been attacked, or vice versa. There was always that kind of situation. Racial situations in New York are not a new phenomena. They always existed to some extent. So we'd have block fights, and you had to be careful where you went and when.

The University Settlement offered social activities, athletics. We used to play basketball there. They would put on shows. In those days I was pretty good at recita-tion, and I recited there and I won some prizes. I read poems like "Gunga Din," "Billy the Kid," and an interesting thing happened. There was something called Boy's Week. And I was asked to recite poems on WOR Radio located in Bamberger's Department Store in Newark. I recited them on the radio, which was in its infancy.[58]

Social workers—whether working in settlement houses, teaching evening classes, or volunteering at Ellis Island—were a priceless resource and comfort to immigrants. The opportunities they created and the hope they offered saved countless numbers of immigrants from unkind fates.

World War II to the Present

When the United States entered World War II in December 1941 after the bombing of Pearl Harbor by the Japanese, many enemy ships were trapped in American waters. Their crews were captured, and, as had happened during World War I, temporarily imprisoned on Ellis Island. The great immigrant surges of the late 1800s and 1920s had subsided and Ellis Island's role as a processing center was greatly diminished.

Military enemies were not the only aliens imprisoned on the island during this period. The Immigration and Naturalization Service and the Federal Bureau of Investigation conducted a nationwide sweep of aliens who were determined to be a possible threat to American security because of their nationalities or political views and arrested or interned these persons, along with their families, in stations around the country. Ellis Island was one of these stations. Thousands of German, Italian, and Japanese citizens living in the United States were rounded up and interned for months and sometimes years. By May 1942, over one thousand enemy aliens were imprisoned on Ellis Island; overcrowding became so extreme that many had to be transferred to dormitories on Riker's Island in the East River.

The population of enemy aliens changed frequently on the island; some were sent there on a temporary basis to await hearings, some were waiting to be transferred to other stations, and some were awaiting deportation.

An Anonymous Story

One woman's three-and-a-half-year ordeal highlights the red tape many aliens faced. Although her husband was an American citizen, she was considered an enemy alien because of her German descent. After being sent to Ellis Island on July 7, 1942, for a short stay she was transferred to another detention center in Gloucester City, New Jersey, until February 1945. She was then sent back to Ellis Island, where she narrowly escaped deportation:

> After the war in Europe had ended in May 1945 we, my fellow internees and I, thought we would be released. But, instead, we all received deportation papers.
>
> In August 1945 I had another hearing at Ellis Island, but I realized that they [the government officials] really were not interested in what I had to say but that they wanted to get rid of me and ship me back to Germany. People who had hearings before and after me were being released but I was still there. Then in October 1945 my name appeared again on the list for a hearing. I told the Ellis Island official that I had had my hearing, he said, "We know, but this time, see to it that your husband is there also."
>
> Then I went to my typewriter and in several pages for the first time I put down what I had to say, instead of being asked silly questions as before.

Ellis Island served as a detention center for enemy aliens during World War II. A *New York Times* reporter visited the center and described a typical day for those being held. Pamela Reeves includes an excerpt from the 1942 *Times* article in her book *Ellis Island: Gateway to the American Dream.*

"Their guards march them to breakfast in the big dining room at 7:30, Germans and Italians together, Japs separately. Dinner is at 12, outdoor exercise begins at 3 if they want it, supper at 5:15 and taps at 10. It leaves a good deal of time to be got through somehow, and the immigration officials do their best to keep the time from hanging too heavily.

Their guests are allowed all the newspapers and magazines they want. They draw on the island library as often as they like. The American Tract Society has stocked it with some 20,000 volumes in about 30 languages. Subject to censorship, they write and receive letters. They telephone under strict supervision. They receive visits from wives, business partners, lawyers, and others whom they have legitimate reasons for seeing."

When the hearing began, they again started with the same type of questions, like, "What did you think when Hitler marched into Czechoslovakia?" I put a copy of my story before each of the three officials presiding at the hearing (one from Immigration and Naturalization Service, one from the State Department, and another fellow who was asking all of the questions). When something came up which I had addressed in my appeal I just said to the three, "I have answered this in my letter," forcing them to at least read it.

On August 20, 1945, I set up an appeal to President Truman from the women internees of Ellis Island. This appeal asked the President to reunite us with our families, from whom we have been separated for several years. Christmas 1945 was nearing and still nothing had happened.

On December 22, 1945, just three days before Christmas, I was called by an Ellis Island official. When I came to him he had several papers in his hand, he said, "Mrs. T. please sit down," at that moment I knew I was going to be released. Then he said, "You are being released, when do you want to leave the Island?" I replied, "With the 4 o'clock ferry."

I did not laugh, I did not cry, I kept myself in check, I had prepared myself for this moment. I left Ellis Island with the 4 o'clock ferry. Finally, the nightmare of three and one-half years was over.[59]

Public Health Service employees, doctors and nurses, and American military personnel and members of the U.S. Coast Guard were also stationed on the island. As happened during World War I, the military virtually occupied the entire island. Renovations were made to the island's hospitals and they were used as military facilities to treat returning American servicemen. Ellis Island was once again busy and productive.

After the War

When the fighting ended in the summer of 1945, the remaining imprisoned aliens and military personnel began to leave. The costs of operating a now-vacant Ellis Island were enormous. Federal authorities began discussing the possibility of shutting down the island or turning it over to another government department, but no one could suggest a practical use for it.

The Public Health Service

The marine hospital remained open until 1951, operated mostly by the Public Health Service. It was used to treat the few immigrants who arrived (many were tuberculosis cases), military personnel, and Coast Guardsmen. In addition, in the years 1945–1951 psychiatric testing, neuropsychiatric services, and electroconvulsive therapy on military personnel and Coast Guardsmen were conducted

After WWII no practical use for Ellis Island could be suggested, and the island became run-down with weeds growing through the buildings.

The Last Child to Live on the Island

Bill Baker, son of psychiatrist James Baker, lived on Ellis Island for two years as a young boy. In Peter Coan's book *Ellis Island Interviews*, he recalls the family's unusual lifestyle.

"My mother viewed Ellis Island as an experience. My father viewed it as an adventure. It certainly was an unusual situation, and it did have its frustrations. Shopping was a little awkward. My mother did all her shopping at the army base on Governor's Island. That's where we went for most things. We ate all our meals at home. Maybe once or twice in the cafeteria, but since this was a hospital environment, I was restricted to a large degree in terms of where I could go and what patients I could be around. I was not allowed on the side of the island where the Great Hall was. I don't recall what all the reasons were, contagious diseases or something.

But it was fascinating, living where we did and being able to view the skyline of New York City and the Statue of Liberty from our backyard. I remember watching the great ocean liners; the Queen Mary, the Queen Elizabeth. I could recognize them by how many smokestacks they had and the fireboats that would escort them with long shooting streams of water. To me that was just a very fascinating experience, and to ride the ferryboat to school on Governor's Island, which was an army base.

I went there for kindergarten and first grade. I had to make the trek into Manhattan on the Ellis Island ferry, which was incredibly slow. I remember that. I remember always being embarrassed by the Ellis Island ferry. It was the worst of any of the ferries in New York Harbor in terms of being slow and ugly. It was an awful army-green-colored boat and it seemed to take forever, but I was fascinated by it. Then, from Manhattan, I would take the ferry out to Governor's Island and walk to the other side of the island to get to school. I was escorted by one of my father's mental patients, a relatively harmless one, named Tom Trimble. He was a merchant seaman who was there at the Marine Hospital and I can think of a couple others. One of them was Charlie. I remember Tom always telling me to stay away from Charlie, 'Watch out for Charlie. He is crazy.'"

during this time. Thorazine, a new drug used to treat schizophrenia and other mental disorders, was tested on many patients at Ellis Island during these years.

Psychiatrist James Baker, his wife, and his son, Bill, were the last family to live on Ellis Island. They left in 1951 after the hospital was finally closed and the island staff was reduced to a skeleton crew. Bill recalls his lonely existence in the rundown buildings:

I remember my father would take me on tours of the hospital, various wards; particularly on Sundays when he was the only doctor and he would make his rounds. I remember the long hallways we had to go down that sometimes got flooded by rain. I remember the offices and the nurses and one nurse named Miss Brave. She was almost like a second mother to me. She was the head nurse. She lived on Long Island somewhere. And I became attached to her, and she became attached to me like an aunt or a grandmother.

When we left in 1951, the Public Health Service had made the decision to close the Marine Hospital. We left for my dad to take another assignment. I don't remember leaving, but I do know we were the last family that was a resident on the island.[60]

The McCarthy Era

The early 1950s were a turbulent time in the nation's history. Senator Joseph McCarthy led hearings to prosecute suspected members of the Communist Party. Eminent businessmen, politicians, and Hollywood celebrities all came under attack. Postwar paranoia concerning national security was rampant. Ellis Island again played a role as a detention center for aliens and immigrants, and the Coast Guard was once again stationed on the island. Mel Berger, a Guardsman during the McCarthy era, recalls his duties: "The main function of the Coast Guard on Ellis Island was to guard the piers of New York, and Hoboken [and] Jersey City. . . . It was making certain that the people were not going to sabotage anything in New York Harbor."[61]

Ellis Island once again became a detention center for visitors and immigrants suspected of being communists during Senator Joseph McCarthy's prosecution.

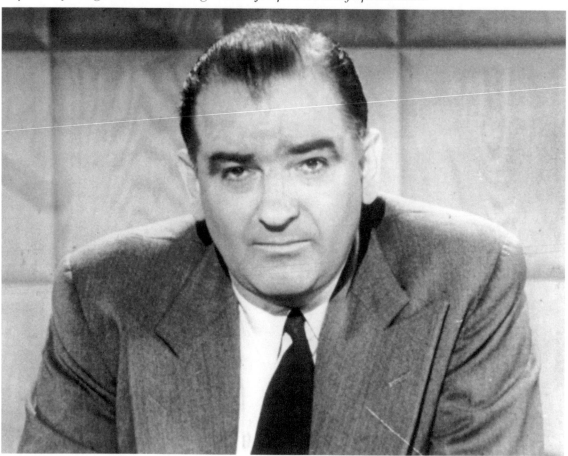

The Internal Security Act

Visitors and immigrants were required to endure long delays and detentions on Ellis Island as they were investigated for Communist affiliations related to their World War II activities. In September 1950 the Internal Security Act was passed, barring all aliens who had been or were currently a member of totalitarian organizations from immigrating. Such aliens already in the country were deported or denied citizenship. The law was strictly enforced. Overcrowding once again became a problem when mass arrests of illegal resident aliens in June 1951 boosted the Ellis Island population to fifteen hundred. A few hasty renovations and repairs were effected, new furniture purchased, and dusty unused rooms were opened to accommodate the detainees. The dining room cafeteria reopened to provide food for the throng of people.

George Voskovec, a Czechoslovakian playwright and actor detained on the island in 1951 under the Internal Security Act, recalled his stay and the irony of being imprisoned by the country most known for upholding individual freedom:

> The Russians have long made heavy propaganda use of Ellis Island. They call it a concentration camp, which, of course, is outrageous. No one mistreats us here. Our jailors—nearly all of them, anyway—are very kindly people, who go to extraordinary lengths, within the system, for which they don't pretend to be responsible, to make our stay here as little like a nightmare as they can. There is a movie here every Tuesday and Thursday night; the children get milk six times a day and go to school three hours a day. We are kept warm and fed generously—nothing like the Colony, I assure you, but more than enough. And, as people are always pointing out to us, it doesn't cost us anything. But I will tell you, it is hard not to be depressed at the realization that within the American government, which has rightly been honored so long as the guardian of individual freedom and human dignity, there is one small agency that can seize a man and bring him to this place, where every day of his life he can look on the mocking face of the Statue of Liberty and where—almost as if this were that other kind of world, behind the Curtain—he is walled in by silence. He isn't told the particulars of his offense, his accusers are nameless, and the weeks and months pass, as if human beings were no more to be considered than cyphers in a manila folder.[62]

As Communist paranoia lessened, officials sought ways to simplify the screening process and eliminate lengthy detentions. In November 1954, a new policy sounded the death knell for Ellis Island; all detainees whose papers were unsatisfactory due to technicalities would be freed on a parole system, and only the few actually determined as possible threats to national security would be locked up in quarters in New York City. The island emptied immediately.

The Last Detainee

The dilapidated unused buildings became mere shadows of their former glory. Government officials estimated that $800,000 to $900,000 could be saved annually by shutting down the facility completely. Attorney General Herbert Brownell discussed his final decision to close Ellis Island during a speech

On November 12, 1954, Ellis Island closed down and was left abandoned and dilapidated for almost twenty-two years.

before thousands of newly naturalized citizens. After giving due credit to the island's prestigious history, he stated, "But today the little island between the Statue of Liberty and the skyline and piers of New York seems to have served its purpose for immigration."[63]

Without ceremony the island shut down operations on November 12, 1954. The last detainee to leave was a Norwegian sailor, Arne Peterssen, who had jumped ship, been held for three days on Ellis Island, and was released on parole to return to Norway. The remaining staff then took its last ride to Bat-

tery Park aboard the Ellis Island ferry. The island remained empty for a decade.

A National Monument

On May 11, 1965, President Lyndon Johnson proclaimed Ellis Island a historic site and part of the Statue of Liberty National Monument, to be administered by the National Park Service. The Statue of Liberty, located a mere seventeen hundred feet to the southeast of Ellis Island, and the buildings on Ellis

Island itself, were in need of repair. However, regardless of the president's proclamation, no federal funds were allocated for either monument. Public monies that could possibly have been appropriated for a restoration project were channeled into the Vietnam War effort.

Weeds and vines climbed the brick walls of Ellis Island's many buildings and invaded the interiors through broken windows. The structures continued to deteriorate; plaster fell onto flooded floorboards and birds, coming in through the windows and gaping rafters, made their home indoors. The long corridors and silent rooms lay in ruins. Ellis Island, the national monument, was nothing more than an empty promise. Louis Sillen, who worked in the Boarding Division on Ellis Island during World War II and after, recalls the island's glory days with sadness:

A Tribute to the Immigrant

In his book *The American People,* Bernard Weisberger reprints a stirring and touching tribute to the immigrant entitled "The Immigrant, an Asset and a Liability" written by Missouri journalist Frederic J. Haskin and originally published in 1913.

"I am the immigrant.

Since the dawn of creation my restless feet have beaten new paths across the earth.

My uneasy bark has tossed on all seas.

My wanderlust was born of the craving for more liberty and a better wage for the sweat of my face.

I looked towards the United States with eyes kindled by the fire of ambition and heart quickened with a new-born hope.

I approached its gates with great expectation.

I entered in fine hope.

I have shouldered my burden as the American man-of-all-work.

I contribute eighty-five per cent of all labor in the slaughtering and meatpacking industries.

I do seven-tenths of the bituminous coal mining.

I do seventy-eight per cent of all the work in the woolen mills.

I contribute nine-tenths of all the labor in the cotton mills.

I make nineteen-twentieths of all the clothing.

I manufacture more than half the shoes.

I build four-fifths of all the furniture.

I make half of the collars, cuffs and shirts.

I turn out four-fifths of all the leather.

I make half the gloves.

I refine nearly nineteen-twentieths of the sugar.

I make half of the tobacco and cigars.

And yet, I am the great American problem.

When I pour out my blood on your altar of labor, and lay down my life as a sacrifice to your god of toil, men make no more comment than at the fall of a sparrow.

But my brawn is woven into the warp and woof of the fabric of your national being.

My children shall be your children and your land shall be my land because my sweat and my blood will cement the foundation of the America of Tomorrow."

[After the closing in 1954] . . . they let it fall down. It was a shame because we had built it up to such a beautiful place. Prior to that we had painted the whole place, always kept it clean, always up to date. We had the most gorgeous grounds that you could want. They called it a country club. The passengers themselves, or I should say, the aliens themselves.[64]

By 1968 the National Park Service was developing a plan for modest preservation of the island. Roof repairs were made, but little else was achieved. In August of that year the Ellis Island ferry, which had transported millions to their new home, sank in its berth. The island once again lay dormant.

Attempted Takeovers

On March 16, 1970, a group of militant Native Americans set out from the New Jersey shore at dawn to take over the island to publicize the plight of the Indian. Their plan was to use the island as a center of Indian culture, but their boat became disabled before ever reaching the island and they were apprehended by the Coast Guard.

A few months later, on July 20, sixty-four members of the National Economic Growth and Reconstruction Organization (NEGRO) moved onto the island. They announced their purpose was to demonstrate that "society's forgotten drug addicts, multigenerational welfare recipients, and former prison inmates" could "create a self-supporting, productive, rehabilitative community."[65] Their goal was to develop a rehabilitation center on the island that would accommodate twenty-five hundred former addicts, convicts, and their families. NEGRO members stayed twelve days and were granted a five-year

special-use permit from the National Park Service for their proposed endeavor. The plan failed, however, and the permit was revoked in 1973.

The First Restoration Effort

In 1974 the Restore Ellis Island Committee was formed to lobby Congress for funds to rehabilitate Ellis Island in time for the nation's upcoming bicentennial celebration in 1976. President Gerald Ford signed a bill on January 1, 1976, appropriating $1 million to repair the main building and another $500,000 to the National Park Service to run the site.

The main building was immediately made safe for visitors and officially reopened to the public on May 28. Six separate one-hour tours led by Park Service rangers were conducted daily. Visitors toured the dilapidated main building following the route immigrants had taken for processing. These tours continued sporadically throughout the ensuing years but no further improvements were made to the main building. In July 1981, *New York Times* writer Sidney H. Schanberg reported on its sad condition:

This one had been shored up and rendered safe, but it is mouldering. Interior walls have crumbled. Mounds of fallen plaster and pools of rainwater from leaking roofs spread darkly across some of the floors. Dust and peeling paint are the most benign signs of the slow rot. Windows are out, and in one room moss and small trees are growing, and pigeons have settled in. Here and there bits of salvaged old furniture have been arranged forlornly in an attempt to recapture the era.[66]

Children touring the main building on Ellis Island.

Schanberg also suggested the possibility of a public fund-raising campaign dedicated to the restoration of the island. In fact, such plans were already being discussed.

A Partnership with Lady Liberty

The Department of the Interior was considering launching a public-private partnership to raise restoration funds for both Ellis Island and the Statue of Liberty in conjunction with Lady Liberty's upcoming centennial birthday in 1986. The proposal was to seek funding entirely from public sources, to be administered by the private sector, and to contract the restoration work through a private foundation, which would presumably accomplish the task much more quickly than government agencies.

In 1982 Lee Iacocca, a Chrysler executive whose own parents had come through Ellis Island, was approached to head the project.

World War II to the Present

The restoration of the Statue of Liberty.

He accepted and, along with a large group of prominent Americans, the Statue of Liberty/Ellis Island Foundation was formed in May of that year. President Ronald Reagan, in naming Iacocca head of the foundation, spoke of the significance of the immigrant experience in American history:

> I can't help but believe—you can call it mysticism, if you will—that God must have placed this land here between the two oceans to be found by a certain kind of people, that whatever corner of the world they came from they had the courage and the desire for freedom that went with it to uproot themselves and come to this strange land.[67]

Objectives of the National Park Service

While the Statue of Liberty/Ellis Island Foundation would be responsible for fund-raising and contracting construction, the National Park Service would be in charge of approving restoration plans. The NPS defined its objectives as:

1. To preserve the Ellis Island complex and return the buildings to active life by devoting major historic structures to public use and interpretation and by making the contributing structures available for adaptive use.

2. To preserve the interiors of the major historic structures on Ellis Island and, through tours and programs, recall the human drama that occurred within these walls and explore the far-reaching effects it had on our nation.

3. To preserve the thousands of artifacts

that are extant on Ellis Island and those that have been donated by families of immigrants to develop a collection that will record and help convey the Ellis Island story.[68]

The island was divided into two zones: the northern, which contained the most historically significant buildings, and the southern, which contained support buildings. The northern zone was designated for restoration first. Fund-raising efforts were successful and by 1984 work was begun.

Restoration

The first order of business was to remove debris from the Great Hall and begin the drying-out process. To avoid buckling and warping of the massive walls, moisture had to be removed slowly. Two large heaters were placed outside the building and pressurized dry air was pumped through its interior. This process took almost two years to complete.

Meanwhile, the exterior limestone was cleaned, the roof replaced, and the ornamental domes were repaired and covered with new copper, as the original copper had been stripped by vandals. A new steel and glass canopy was built at the entrance which echoed the original design. All metalwork was painted "Ellis Island red."

The Great Hall

Once the interior of the main building was stabilized, restoration to its 1918 to 1924 appearance began—that is, to the time during which the vaulted Guastavino ceiling had been constructed in the Great Hall. The Great Hall was to be the centerpiece of the

By 1984, restoration on Ellis Island began.

restoration. Miraculously, and to the credit of the workmen who had done the original installation, only 27 of the 28,282 tiles needed to be repaired or replaced.

During the restoration process, removal of layers of peeling paint revealed graffiti scrawled by immigrants, particularly evident in the detention and waiting rooms. Most was inscribed in pencil or in the blue chalk that inspectors had used. Initials, names, dates, cartoons, flowers, religious symbols, and comments were found; all were restored to be put on display as exhibits.

When refitting the various rooms, original fixtures were used whenever possible, including 37 sinks, 190 radiators, and 51 toilets. In the Dormitory Room, triple-tiered bunks stand as reminders of the grim accommodations the immigrants faced.

Family Ties

For many of those involved in the restoration process, Ellis Island was a part of their family history. Victor Demianycz, a machinist who worked on the restoration, remembered the emotions evoked on his first day of work:

My mom came over from the Ukraine before World War I. She was the oldest of four sisters, and came to Ellis Island at the age of sixteen. Nowadays, a sixteen-year-old can't even cross the street, no less travel around the world by herself. At dinnertime, she would talk about her early years in this country, and described how scared she was when she arrived at Ellis and saw all those people in the Great Hall.

The first day I came to work at Ellis, I stood in the Great Hall and wondered what it was like for my mother.[69]

The Museum Opens

After nearly eight years of work and close to $160 million, most in private-sector donations, Ellis Island—the largest restoration project attempted to date—was once again opened to the public in September 1990. Over 40 percent of Americans can trace their ancestry back to family members who came through Ellis Island. Their stories remain

After eight years and $160 million, Ellis Island made its numerous exhibits open to the public.

alive in the museum exhibits made possible by numerous individuals who donated hundreds of belongings and family treasures displayed along with the many historical artifacts uncovered during the restoration.

The restored main building and renewed grounds and landscape welcome visitors as they disembark from ferries onto the island as millions of immigrants did before them. On the grounds stands a statue sculpted by Jeanne Rynhart of Annie Moore, the first immigrant processed on the island. The statue was a gift to the American people from the Irish American Cultural Institute.

Once inside the main building, tours begin in the Baggage Room, where steamer trunks, suitcases, and baskets once used by immigrants are on display. Visitors must then climb a reconstructed staircase to reach the first floor just as immigrants did while doctors scrutinized their progress looking for possible medical problems.

Permanent exhibits occupy over forty thousand square feet—landing cards, ships' manifests, and passports are on display along with hundreds of cherished objects, photographs, and family papers immigrants brought with them from their homelands. Throughout the building, loudspeakers broadcast recordings of immigrants telling their stories of Ellis Island and their immigration experience.

The Registry Room, or Great Hall, contains historic benches and reproductions of the tall inspection desks the immigrants stood before during their legal inspections. Lighting the space are two huge restored brass and glass chandeliers (a third is a reproduction). Visitors may also go to the Dormitory Room; the Railroad Ticket Office, which contains a history of immigration exhibit; and the room

The American Immigrant Wall of Honor

On the official Ellis Island website, organizer Lee Iacocca tells what the American Immigrant Wall of Honor means to him.

"Restoring Ellis Island has been a labor of love for me. Both of my parents came through there. My dad for the first time in 1902 and then again 19 years later to bring back a bride—my mother. They used to tell me about Ellis. The island really became a part of my being.

I often wonder where I would be and what I would be doing if my parents had decided to remain in Italy. I'm sure my life would have taken a far different turn if it were not for Nicola and Antoinette Iacocca and their pursuit of the American dream.

My gratitude for the opportunities they gave me inspired the creation of The American Immigrant Wall of Honor. I'm proud to have their names inscribed as a tribute to their contribution to the building of this nation. I'm also very pleased that so many Americans have joined me in honoring their ancestors—over 500,000 names are currently inscribed, and new registrations are coming in everyday. It's not just for those who came through Ellis Island—it honors all of America's immigrants who came to this great Melting Pot in search of freedom and opportunity."

The Wall of Honor contains over 500,000 names of immigrants, making it the largest wall of names and representing virtually every nationality in the world.

where the Board of Special Inquiry heard cases.

The Wall of Honor

One of the most popular exhibits, the American Immigrant Wall of Honor, stands as a tribute to all American immigrants regardless of when they immigrated or which port they came through. The 653-foot-long wall is the largest wall of names in the world; over 500,000 names are inscribed and additions are still being made. Donors contributing $100 or more may have their relatives' names engraved as a tribute. Virtually every nation-

ality on earth is represented and the name engravings have raised over $50 million for improvements to the island. Stephen Briganti of the Statue of Liberty/Ellis Island Foundation stated that the names not only raised a lot of money, but also "indicate that the American people want to make sure their symbols are taken care of."[70]

Still Controversial

In 1998, Ellis Island was once again a center of controversy in New York State and New Jersey as the question of ownership was brought to the courts. New Jersey won the case as the Supreme Court ruled that most of Ellis Island is actually inside New Jersey boundaries. The decision did not sit well with New York mayor Rudolph Giuliani, who said that the Court

> is still not going to convince me that my grandfather, when he was sitting in Italy thinking about coming to the United States, getting on the ship in Genoa, was saying, "I'm coming to New Jersey." He was coming to the streets of New York. That's why everybody will always believe . . . that all of Ellis Island is actually part of New York.[71]

Columbia University historian James Shelton, who spoke on behalf of New Jersey's claim, summed up his feelings about the squabble by saying, "We ought to start thinking of immigration as the classic American experience. In our blood runs the blood of the people who created the experience. It doesn't belong to any one state."[72]

The story of Ellis Island is an indelible part of America's past. It is a poignant and powerful reminder of the immigrants who helped shape the country. And now, as a national monument, Ellis Island serves as a proud testament to its own history.

Notes

Introduction: Island of Hope, Island of Tears

1. Quoted in James B. Bell and Richard I. Abrams, *In Search of Liberty: The Story of the Statue of Liberty and Ellis Island.* New York: Doubleday, 1984, p. 58.
2. Quoted in Mary J. Shapiro, *Ellis Island: An Illustrated History of the Immigrant Experience.* New York: Macmillan, 1991, p. 121.
3. Quoted in David M. Brownstone, Irene M. Frank, and Douglass L. Brownstone, *Island of Hope, Island of Tears.* New York: Rawson, Wade, 1979, p. 147.

Chapter 1: Coming to America

4. Quoted in R. Conrad Stein, *Ellis Island.* Chicago: Childrens Press, 1992, p. 8.
5. Quoted in Stein, *Ellis Island,* p. 10.
6. Quoted in Shirley Blumenthal, *Coming to America,* New York: Delacorte Press, 1981, p. 85.
7. Quoted in Edward Oxford, "Hope, Tears, and Remembrance," *American History Illustrated,* September/October 1990, p. 28.
8. Quoted in Oxford, "Hope, Tears, and Remembrance."
9. Quoted in Peter Morton Coan, *Ellis Island Interviews: In Their Own Words.* New York: Facts On File, 1977, p. 277.
10. Quoted in Shapiro, *Ellis Island,* p. 169.
11. Quoted in Shapiro, *Ellis Island,* p. 165.
12. Quoted in Virginia Yans-McLaughlin and Marjorie Lightman, *Ellis Island and the Peopling of America.* New York: New Press, 1997, p. 142.
13. Quoted in Shapiro, *Ellis Island,* p. 115.

14. Quoted in Thomas M. Pitkin, *Keepers of the Gate.* New York: New York University Press, 1975, p. 91.
15. Quoted in Bell and Abrams, *In Search of Liberty,* p. 93.
16. Quoted in Susan Jonas, ed., *Ellis Island: Echoes from a Nation's Past.* New York: Aperture Foundation, 1989, p. 86.
17. Quoted in Ellen Levine, *If Your Name Was Changed at Ellis Island.* New York: Scholastic, 1993, p. 43.
18. Oxford, "Hope, Tears, and Remembrance."
19. Quoted in Bernard A. Weisberger, *The American People.* New York: American Heritage, 1971, p. 283.

Chapter 2: Those Who Were Detained

20. Shapiro, *Ellis Island,* p. 144.
21. Quoted in Wilson S. Tifft, *Ellis Island.* Chicago: Contemporary Books, 1990, p. 75.
22. Quoted in Weisberger, *The American People,* p. 279.
23. Quoted in Yans-McLaughlin and Lightman, *Ellis Island and the Peopling of America,* p. 66.
24. Quoted in Tifft, *Ellis Island,* p. 87.
25. Quoted in Roger Daniels, *Coming to America.* New York: HarperCollins, 1990, p. 273.
26. Ellis Island website, http://members.aol.com/EllisNJ/texts/IRpt1.htm.
27. Quoted in Pamela Reeves, *Ellis Island: Gateway to the American Dream.* New York: Crescent Books, 1991, p. 68.
28. Quoted in Coan, *Ellis Island Interviews,* p. 137.

29. Quoted in Shapiro, *Ellis Island,* p. 135.
30. Quoted in Shapiro, *Ellis Island,* p. 135.
31. Quoted in Coan, *Ellis Island Interviews,* p. 164.
32. Quoted in Shapiro, *Ellis Island,* p. 137.

Chapter 3: Daily Life on the Island

33. Quoted in Tifft, *Ellis Island,* p. 78.
34. Quoted in Reeves, *Ellis Island,* p. 106.
35. Quoted in Shapiro, *Ellis Island,* p. 145.
36. Quoted in Oxford, "Hope, Tears, and Remembrance."
37. Quoted in Shapiro, *Ellis Island,* p. 151.
38. Quoted in Edward Corsi, *In the Shadow of Liberty.* New York: Arno Press, 1969, p. 293.
39. Quoted in Shapiro, *Ellis Island,* p. 154.
40. Quoted in Ann Novotny, *Strangers at the Door.* Riverside, CT: Chatham Press, 1971, p. 73.
41. Quoted in Reeves, *Ellis Island,* p. 44.
42. Quoted in Tifft, *Ellis Island,* p. 87.
43. Quoted in Corsi, *In the Shadow of Liberty,* p. 121.
44. Quoted in Pitkin, *Keepers of the Gate,* p. 68.
45. Quoted in Novotny, *Strangers at the Door,* p. 75.
46. Quoted in Novotny, *Strangers at the Door,* p. 75.
47. Quoted in Reeves, *Ellis Island,* p. 48.
48. Quoted in Tifft, *Ellis Island,* p. 89.
49. Quoted in Reeves, *Ellis Island,* p. 92.
50. Quoted in Shapiro, *Ellis Island,* p. 150.
51. Quoted in Corsi, *In the Shadow of Liberty,* p. 92.
52. Quoted in Shapiro, *Ellis Island,* p. 150.

53. Quoted in Shapiro, *Ellis Island,* p. 156.
54. Quoted in Oxford, "Hope, Tears, and Remembrance."

Chapter 4: Immigrant Aid Societies

55. Quoted in Shapiro, *Ellis Island,* p. 159.
56. Ellis Island website, http://members.aol.com/EllisIsNJ/private/ellis.htm.
57. Quoted in Pitkin, *Keepers of the Gate,* p. 78.
58. Quoted in Coan, *Ellis Island Interviews,* p. 77.

Chapter 5: World War II to the Present

59. Ellis Island website, http://www.netzone.com/~adjacobs/ellis.html.
60. Quoted in Coan, *Ellis Island Interviews,* p. 21.
61. Quoted in Coan, *Ellis Island Interviews,* p. 33.
62. Quoted in Jonas, *Ellis Island,* p. 62.
63. Quoted in Tifft, *Ellis Island,* p. 133.
64. Quoted in Tifft, *Ellis Island,* p. 159.
65. Quoted in Tifft, *Ellis Island,* p. 165.
66. Quoted in Tifft, *Ellis Island,* p. 171.
67. Quoted in Tifft, *Ellis Island,* p. 172.
68. Quoted in Tifft, *Ellis Island,* p. 175.
69. Quoted in Jonas, *Ellis Island,* p. 98.
70. Quoted in Rebecca Cook, "Writing on Ellis Island Wall Coming to End," *Newsday,* March 13, 1995.
71. Quoted in Martha T. Moore, "To Immigrants It Was Simply 'America,'" *USA Today,* May 27, 1998.
72. Quoted in Moore, "To Immigrants It Was Simply 'America.'"

For Further Reading

Shirley Blumenthal, *Coming to America.* New York: Delacorte Press, 1981. Detailed study of circumstances in eastern Europe that spawned mass emigration and of the difficult struggle immigrants faced in America after their arrival and successful passage through Ellis Island.

Willard A. Heaps, *The Story of Ellis Island.* New York: Seabury Press, 1967. Excellent book detailing various aspects of immigration from the voyage in steerage to the examinations and conditions the immigrants faced once they reached the island.

Steven Kroll, *Ellis Island: Doorway to Freedom.* New York: Holiday House, 1995. Easy-to-read, detailed account of the immigrant experience on Ellis Island.

Erik V. Krustrup, *Gateway to America: New York City.* Mankato, MN: Creative Education, 1982. Excellent account of the Ellis Island immigration process and the immigrants' lives after arriving in New York City.

Ellen Levine, *If Your Name Was Changed at Ellis Island.* New York: Scholastic, 1993. Excellent overview of all aspects of Ellis Island, including the help available to immigrant detainees.

R. Conrad Stein, *Ellis Island.* Chicago: Childrens Press, 1992. An easy-to-read overview of Ellis Island, focusing on the immigrants' arrival and the adjustments to American life immigrants faced after entry to the mainland.

Wilton Tifft and Thomas Dunne, *Ellis Island.* New York: W. W. Norton, 1971. A photographic history containing many excellent photos of the massive deterioration of Ellis Island that took place during the years before restoration.

Works Consulted

Books

James B. Bell and Richard I. Abrams, *In Search of Liberty: The Story of the Statue of Liberty and Ellis Island*. New York: Doubleday, 1984. A detailed account of the construction of the Statue of Liberty and Ellis Island.

Christian Blanchet and Bertrand Dard, *Statue of Liberty: The First Hundred Years*. New York: American Heritage, 1985. A comprehensive history of the Statue of Liberty interspersed with information on the immigrant experience at Ellis Island.

David M. Brownstone, Irene M. Frank, and Douglass L. Brownstone, *Island of Hope, Island of Tears*. New York: Rawson, Wade, 1979. Fact-filled overview of the immigration experience including many quotations and anecdotes from immigrants and employees.

Peter Morton Coan, *Ellis Island Interviews: In Their Own Words*. New York: Facts On File, 1997. Over one hundred oral histories related by immigrants and employees of Ellis Island.

Edward Corsi, *In the Shadow of Liberty*. New York: Arno Press, 1969. The fascinating personal reflections of a former commissioner of Ellis Island.

Roger Daniels, *Coming to America*. New York: HarperCollins, 1990. A complete overview of the history of immigration from colonial times to the present.

Oscar Handlin, *A Pictorial History of Immigration*. New York: Crown, 1972. A pictorial history of American immigration from the nomadic Indians of the 1600s to Cuban refugees of the 1960s.

Susan Jonas, ed., *Ellis Island: Echoes from a Nation's Past*. New York: Aperture Foundation, 1989. Well-done photoessay with collected personal histories.

Ann Novotny, *Strangers at the Door*. Riverside, CT: Chatham Press, 1971. Complete history of Ellis Island with good final chapter on its deterioration and closing.

Thomas M. Pitkin, *Keepers of the Gate*. New York: New York University Press, 1975. Detailed book with good focus on political aspects and problems of running the island.

Pamela Reeves, *Ellis Island: Gateway to the American Dream*. New York: Crescent Books, 1991. Excellent account of Ellis Island history and the social reform and immigration laws that altered it throughout the years.

Mary J. Shapiro, *Ellis Island: An Illustrated History of the Immigrant Experience*. New York: Macmillan, 1991. In-depth account of the peak years of immigration and of daily life on the island.

Wilton S. Tifft, *Ellis Island*. Chicago: Contemporary Books, 1990. Detailed informative pictorial account of the immigrants and the many buildings of Ellis Island in which they were processed and housed.

Bernard A. Weisberger, *The American People*. New York: American Heritage, 1971. In-depth social history of the problems and prejudices faced by immigrants and the trials they endured on Ellis Island.

Virginia Yans-McLaughlin and Marjorie Lightman, *Ellis Island and the Peopling of America*. New York: New Press, 1997. Detailed account of U.S. immigration policy filled with statistics and Ellis Island history.

Periodicals

Rebecca Cook, "Writing on Ellis Island Wall Coming to End", *Newsday*, March 13, 1995. Article on the Wall of Honor, which bears the inscribed names of over 495,000 immigrants.

Judie Glave, "Ellis Island Opening Its Great Doors Again," *Wichita Eagle*, September 9, 1990. Article on reopening of the island to tourists after $156 million restoration.

Martha T. Moore, "To Immigrants It Was Simply 'America,'" *USA Today*, May 27, 1998. Account of Supreme Court ruling that Ellis Island is New Jersey land.

Edward Oxford, "Hope, Tears, and Remembrance," *American History Illustrated*, September/October 1990. Lengthy article on Ellis Island highlighting the medical examinations and immigration interview process.

Cynthia Owen Philip, "Celebrating an Island Artifact," *Archaeology*, September/October 1990, pp. 45–51. Fascinating account of test excavations conducted during the restoration process.

Websites

http://members.aol.com/EllisIsNJ/private/ellis.htm. This website gives information on the history of the island, recordkeeping of immigrants, and a comprehensive analysis of the recent Supreme Court case between New York and New Jersey over ownership of the island.

http://members.aol.com/EllisNJ/texts/IRpt1.htm. Many aspects of life on the island are covered with detailed information about social welfare work and immigrant aid societies.

http://www.ellisisland.org. The official Ellis Island website covers the museum today and explains the mission of the foundation to preserve the island's heritage.

http://www.netzone.com/~adjacobs/ellis.html. An interesting website that gives detailed information and personal accounts from enemy aliens incarcerated on the island during World War II.

Index

Picture Credits

About the Author

Renee C. Rebman is a published playwright, speaker, actress, director, and an active volunteer at local elementary schools. Renee's first nonfiction book, *Prohibition,* was published by Lucent Books.

She visited Ellis Island in November 1990 and noted in her diary, "was nearly in tears, a wonderful experience. Ellis Island was for me, unforgettable." Her dream of one day writing about the history of the island has been realized with the publication of this book.

Renee lives in Lexington, Ohio, with her daughter, Scarlett, and her son, Roddy.